THE OLD TESTAMENT
IN 12 VERSES

THE OLD TESTAMENT IN 12 VERSES

Brad E. Kelle and
Stephanie Smith Matthews,
Editors

THE FOUNDRY
PUBLISHING

Cover design:Caines Design
Interior design: Sharon Page

Unless otherwise indicated, all Scripture quotations are each author's individual translation.

The following version of Scripture is in the public domain:

The King James Version (KJV)

The following copyrighted versions of Scripture are used by permission:

The ESV® Bible (The Holy Bible, English Standard Version®), copyright © 2001 by Crossway, a publishing ministry of Good News Publishers. All rights reserved.

THE MESSAGE (MSG), copyright © 1993, 2002, 2018 by Eugene H. Peterson. Used by permission of NavPress. All rights reserved. Represented by Tyndale House Publishers.

The New American Standard Bible® (NASB®), copyright © 1960, 1971, 1977, 1995, 2020 by The Lockman Foundation. All rights reserved. www.lockman.org.

The Holy Bible, New International Version® (NIV®). Copyright © 1973, 1978, 1984, 2011 by Biblica, Inc.™ Used by permission of Zondervan. All rights reserved worldwide. www.zondervan.com. The "NIV" and "New International Version" are trademarks registered in the United States Patent and Trademark Office by Biblica, Inc.™

The New King James Version® (NKJV). Copyright © 1982 by Thomas Nelson. All rights reserved.

The Holy Bible, New Living Translation (NLT), copyright © 1996, 2004, 2015 by Tyndale House Foundation. Used by permission of Tyndale House Publishers, Carol Stream, Illinois 60188. All rights reserved.

The New Revised Standard Version Bible (NRSV), copyright © 1989 National Council of the Churches of Christ in the United States of America. All rights reserved worldwide.

Library of Congress Cataloging-in-Publication Data
Names: Kelle, Brad E., 1973- editor. | Matthews, Stephanie Smith, 1988- editor.
Title: The Old Testament in 12 verses / Brad E. Kelle, and Stephanie Smith Matthews, editors.
Other titles: Old Testament in twelve verses
Description: Kansas City, MO : The Foundry Publishing, [2022] | Includes bibliographical references and index. | Summa-ry: "For many, the Old Testament is an unwieldy collection of stories, poems, rituals, and laws. The Old Testament in 12 Verses streamlines a clear path to understanding this first part of the Bible. By exploring 12 Scripture passages, the authors illuminate the major themes of the Old Testament and equip the reader with a sound overview of the Bible's first 39 books"— Provided by publisher.
Identifiers: LCCN 2022024349 (print) | LCCN 2022024350 (ebook) | ISBN 9780834141544 |
    ISBN 9780834141551 (ebook)
Subjects: LCSH: Bible. Old Testament—Introductions.
Classification: LCC BS1140.3 .O43 2022 (print) | LCC BS1140.3 (ebook) | DDC 221.6/1—dc23/eng/20220801
LC record available at https://lccn.loc.gov/2022024349
LC ebook record available at https://lccn.loc.gov/2022024350

The internet addresses, email addresses, and phone numbers in this book are accurate at the time of publi-cation. They are provided as a resource. The Foundry Publishing® does not endorse them or vouch for their content or permanence.

10 9 8 7 6 5 4 3 2 1

CONTENTS

INTRODUCTION
Brad E. Kelle

How can you best get to know the Old Testament? Can you befriend the
Old Testament as you would a person in your life? If so, how? There are
many answers to that question. The long history of biblical interpretation
is filled with helpful approaches and methods meant to give interested
readers ways to understand and articulate what the Old Testament is—
both on the whole and as a whole[1]—and why it matters for Christians.
Some of these look to history, others point to major ideas that span the
biblical books, and still others appeal to the Old Testament's connections
to the New Testament.

   Certainly getting to know the Old Testament has its challenges. It
is big, after all—and often feels untidy and, at times, confusing. Today's
readers often perceive the Old Testament to be an unwieldy collection of
diverse materials that include stories, poems, rituals, genealogies, prayers,
and laws. Then there is the seeming strangeness of some of the texts for
contemporary readers. The culture, practices, and perspectives of ancient

---

1. This two-part phrase defines our approach to the Old Testament. We want readers
to get to know the Old Testament "on the whole"—that is, what it is in its major parts (although there are also minor parts). *And* we want them to get to know it simultaneously "as a
whole"—that is, what it is together as one thing.

Israelites, who lived in a time and place very different from modern Western realities in particular, shine through the biblical writings and confront readers with unusual religious acts, unexpected descriptions of God and the world, and sometimes disconcerting behavior.

Simply put, the Old Testament doesn't give up its fruit easily for today's Christian readers. And for some, it's all just a little too much to get their minds (and hearts!) around. Not surprisingly, there is a long history in the church of discounting the Old Testament as important, even authoritative revelation, for the life and faith of God's people. Some have even claimed the Old Testament should be relegated to an inferior role or altogether unhooked from believers' faith and practice.[2] But even for those who wouldn't go that far, the task of gaining an overall sense of the Old Testament can be a challenging one.

This book aims to help preachers, teachers, and laypersons who want an additional resource for getting to know—maybe even befriending— the Old Testament in order to do the hard but meaningful work of interpretation, proclamation, and ministry. The approach taken here is surely not the only way to understand and articulate what the Old Testament is on the whole and as a whole. But together the chapters in this book seek to introduce the Old Testament in a particular way (although surely not one that is exhaustive or comprehensive). Rather than talking in general terms, overall categories, or abstract descriptions, this book uses twelve

---

2. There is a specific history in the church of discounting the Old Testament when it comes to the proper understanding of God's character, especially in light of the New Testament. In the early centuries of Christianity, the Christian leader Marcion of Sinope (in the second century CE) argued not only that the Old Testament (and much of the New Testament) was irrelevant for Christians but also that the God revealed in the Old Testament was a violent, war-making, lower divine being who was actually an altogether different God from the one revealed in the teachings of Jesus. For a different approach that lifts up portraits of a loving God from various Old Testament texts, see the earlier volume featuring articles from many of the same contributors found in the present book: Brad E. Kelle and Stephanie Smith Matthews, eds., *Encountering the God of Love: Portraits from the Old Testament* (Kansas City: Foundry, 2021).

verses (well, really twelve passages) to get to know the Old Testament as a whole. It does so in much the same way that one might befriend a person by learning about her or his specific interests, traits, passions, and activities and then drawing general conclusions about who that person is. Each chapter explores a specific biblical text with the goal of using that passage to understand better the Old Testament overall. The micro-level of representative passages yields a macro-level sense of the Old Testament as a whole.

More specifically, the studies of the biblical passages in the chapters that follow suggest two vital things about the Old Testament. First, throughout the Old Testament, several major themes occur repeatedly, albeit often in different ways. These themes constitute the most common overall elements of the Old Testament and unite the different biblical writings in important ways. The six themes are as follows:

1. *God's creative and re-creative work.* This theme includes portrayals of creation and new creation, the experience of exile, and the promise of transformation with the imagery of a new heart and new covenant.

2. *God's saving work.* This theme includes the stories of God's saving acts in history done on behalf of Israel (the exodus, wilderness provisions, Sinai covenant, promised land, exile, and restoration).

3. *God's preferences and partners.* This theme includes the Old Testament's affirmations that God works on behalf of the oppressed, poor, and marginalized and works through persons and communities that are often unheralded.

4. *The character and life of the covenant community (with God and each other).* This theme includes texts that describe God's presence among the Israelites in and through the covenant, worship, sacrifice, ritual, and prayer. It also includes the divine call upon Israel to be an instrument of blessing to the world (Gen. 12:1-3), to serve as a holy nation mediating God's presence to others in a priestly manner (Exod. 19; Lev. 19), and to act in undivided loyalty and uncompromised faithfulness to God (Deut. 6:4-5). Here we find the voices of the prophets as they demand that God's

people practice justice and righteousness in the religious, political, social, and economic realities of their day.

5. *Human life and experience in the world.* This theme includes the Old Testament's wisdom texts that not only instruct God's people in how to live a good life before God in the world but also explore questions concerning suffering, God's justness, and lament.

6. *God's ongoing presence in the covenant community and the world, past, present, and future.* This theme includes the depictions of leadership (both good and bad) in ancient Israel (especially through priests and kings) and the activity of the Spirit with God's people.

Equally as important, however, the studies of the specific passages in the chapters that follow show that although the Old Testament writings unite around these major themes, the Old Testament as a whole is a conversation among multiple voices and perspectives that approach and express the themes in different, sometimes divergent, ways. This diversity, while creating some complexity for readers, is vital for getting to know the Old Testament. These biblical writings don't always speak with one voice, even about the most vital of themes. Rather, they show how difference avoids oversimplification, enriches experiences, and provides broader ways of engaging the most crucial elements of life as God's people in the world. Moreover, the ongoing, unsettled conversation around these themes found among the Old Testament writings invites us to join in the conversation about the things addressed. And through the Spirit, that conversation can then become a conversation we have with God, rooted in our own particular contexts in which we encounter Scripture in all of its diversity.

The representative biblical passages come from across every major section of the Old Testament. Some of them are probably expected inclusions in a list like ours; others may be surprising to certain readers. In every case, the study of the passage expounds how each interpreter understands the text and how she or he sees its connections with the Old Testament's larger themes. Each chapter begins by locating the passage in its canonical context within the Old Testament as a whole and then proceeds through the passage with a commentary-style Bible study. The studies are not comprehensive and don't attempt to address every issue that might be relevant for interpretation. In addition to an overall interpretation, the goal is to explore how that specific passage contributes to the Bible's internal conversation about the main themes outlined above and to invite others to reflect on the passage from that perspective with an eye toward their own contexts. With this last goal in mind, each chapter concludes with a "Reflection" designed to foster conversation about the passage and its connections to the larger Old Testament themes, as well as to provide some practical responses that include activities, exercises, prayers, and more.

The goals of this collection reflect the hearts of its editors and contributors. The book that Stephanie Smith Matthews and I previously coedited (*Encountering the God of Love: Portraits from the Old Testament* [Kansas City: Foundry, 2021]) brought together for the first time in a single collection interpretive studies written by those who serve as professors of Old Testament in universities, seminaries, and Bible colleges associated with the Church of the Nazarene, especially within the continental United States and the Philippines. The present collection includes the work of substantially the same group with a few additions, including one who serves in a Canadian context. The idea for the book emerged as this group of Old Testament teachers and scholars met together virtually for conversation and support throughout the months of the global pandemic in 2020. We love the Old Testament (after all, we teach it for a living!). We experience God's presence and grace as we prayerfully study it. And our conversations often turned to how we could encourage and equip our students, as well as preachers, teachers, and laypersons doing the hard work of interpretation, proclamation, and ministry, to approach the Old Testament in meaningful ways that point to its central themes and diverse perspectives.

As in the case of our previous volume, in view of the global nature of the Church of the Nazarene today, the contributors here do not constitute a full representation. Women and men in various parts of Africa, Europe, South America, and other locations teach the Old Testament and contribute academic writings to help both ministers and laypersons. While the contributors to this volume come from several different geographical areas in the United States, Canada, and the Philippines, the limitations in representation and perspective are apparent against the backdrop of a global church. The authors in this book are ten men but only four women, and all but one from the same racial and ethnic background. This is no disqualification of the work contained here. But it is a reminder of who we are at the moment in many of our most established educational institutions.

The diversity in the biblical writings themselves creates a moral imperative to seek the same level of diversity among those who engage the Bible in their various contexts and through the lenses of their own experiences within a global church. The God who became flesh in the person, life, and times of Jesus of Nazareth likewise comes—in the Spirit and through the rich diversity of Scripture's testimony—to encounter the people of God in the midst of their personal, communal, and social realities. Appropriately, then, the authors included in this book do not pretend to objectivity or finality. While limited in their perspectives and contexts, they attempt to offer some of the fruits of academic biblical studies as a resource to all who may take up these biblical texts as preachers, teachers, and readers in the hopes of a more meaningful engagement with the Old Testament.

A couple of caveats may be helpful to note at the outset. Some inconsistencies appear among the chapters—a few of which, at least, are present by design. The editors have not, for instance, standardized all biblical quotations to be from a single version. Rather, we have allowed the individual preferences of the authors and indicated those preferences in the chapters. Individual authors have arranged the discussions of their chosen biblical passages as they saw fit, with some taking a more academic tone or using a more technical approach than others. Hence, some chapters include a number of notes that reference scholarly resources and insights for further study while others proceed in a more informal manner. Without strict uniformity, each author has her or his say in a way that not only allows the reader to hear a particular perspective but also invites further reflection and other insights.

The fervent hope of everyone involved with this volume is that it will provide a resource for preachers, teachers, and laypersons to move toward a better sense of what the Old Testament is and why it matters for Christian life and faith. We want to encourage and equip people to befriend the Old Testament. Twelve representative passages invite readers to consider the Old Testament's major themes, but to do so by engaging the rich diversity with which those themes are articulated. In an increasingly diverse church and world, there is something powerful about Scripture's own diversity as a reflection of God's nature and kingdom. If we are willing, with God's help, to engage the complexity found within Scripture's testimony, we may be more open and better equipped to understand, value, and attend to the diversity found in the lives of those in the church and the world today.

1
GENESIS 12:1
Mitchel Modine and Tsuneki Toyoda

God said to Abram, "Go from your land, from your birthplace,
from the household of your father to the land that I will show you."
—Genesis 12:1

While some people may move from one place to another, others stay
rooted in the same place their entire lives. The idea of moving makes
the biblical story of Abraham significant. The call of Abraham to leave
his homeland and journey to a new one stands at the beginning of one of
the most important life stories in the Bible. It is the journey that makes it
important, because this is the first of many decisions Abraham made in his
life, resulting in later traditions calling him the "father of faith." Indeed,
one might say that Abraham is the human originator of three religious
traditions: Judaism, Christianity, and Islam.[1]

---

1. Two cautions should be noted here. First, it is important to mention that Abraham is
the human originator to uphold, in particular, the role of Jesus in the foundation of Christianity. This is rather to recognize that God has always used human partners to accomplish the
divine mission, a point emphasized by Wesleyan theology. Second, while Abraham is important to all three monotheistic religions, he appears differently in them. For Judaism, Abra-

In this essay, the story of Abraham will help introduce the Old Testament and how it remains important for Christian spirituality. We will discuss several things. First, we will see how our following God is important for God's mission. Here we will answer the question, "What if I don't do what God is calling me to do?" Second, we will see how our following God is important for our lives. Here we will see how taking the Old Testament characters as models of morality can lead to error and misunderstanding. Finally, we will see how our following God is important for the world. Here we will explore the meaning of the phrase "blessed to be a blessing."

Genesis 12:1 in the Old Testament

The biblical tradition remembers Abraham's acts of faithfulness as those which defined "faithfulness": essentially, "faithfulness" meant following God without asking questions. Later biblical tradition, not to mention later theological reflection, tempered this view significantly. Even so, however, Abraham has never faced a serious challenge for his preeminence among faithful persons spoken of in the Bible. Two acts in particular cement Abraham's lofty position: his willingness to follow God to an unseen place and his willingness to sacrifice his son Isaac, whom God had given him as a kind of reward for his first faithful act. These acts are important, even though outside the book of Genesis the Old Testament never again mentions them.[2] For that matter, even the New Testament does not explicitly mention the first act outside of the list of famous faithful folks described in Hebrews 11 (see v. 8), and mention of the second is only later in that same chapter (v. 17) and once in James (2:21). The apostle Paul, however, does make a great deal out of how Abraham was faithful before

ham is the familial ancestor. For Christianity, having been "grafted on to the tree" (Rom. 11:17), Abraham was a spiritual ancestor. For Islam, Ibrahim (the Arabic name) was one of the long line of prophets, incidentally including Jesus (Isa) and culminating in Muḥammad.

2. The books from Exodus to Malachi mention Abraham forty-one times, the vast majority of which occur within the triad of Abraham, Isaac, and Jacob (or Israel).

the giving of the Jewish law (see Rom. 4).[3] Moreover, as we will demonstrate below, Abraham's story of faithfulness was not, as the biblical story admits, a story of complete success without any deviation from the "plan."

Abraham's willingness to follow God, even if not always wholeheartedly, sheds a hopeful light on us and our faith in this difficult situation.

Exploration of this topic seems timely for Christians while the COVID-19 pandemic continues to rage throughout the world, abating in some places and intensifying in others. Christians may legitimately question what effect our following God or our obedience could have on the people and the church in this world and in the future. Abraham's willingness to follow God, even if not always wholeheartedly, sheds a hopeful light on us and our faith in this difficult situation.

Genesis 12:1: What Does It Mean to Follow God?

Jesus's commission to "go and make disciples of all nations" (Matt. 28:19) has fueled extensive missionary efforts throughout the centuries. As for Protestant Christianity, the so-called modern missionary movement began in the nineteenth century.[4] A corollary of this is the sense many feel that God has called them specifically to a specific ministry or to a specific place.

---

3. The New Testament speaks of Abraham sixty-four times, three of which draw on the famous phrase "Abraham believed God, and it was considered righteousness for him" (Gen. 15:6).

4. For a recent discussion, see Dorothy Bullón, "The Missionary Movement of the Nineteenth Century," *Didache: Faithful Teaching* 14, no. 1 (Summer 2014), https://didache.nazarene .org/index.php/volume-14-1/1030-didache-v14n1-07b-19th-cent-missions-bullonen/file.

Michael E. Whelchel's research into the psychological typing of missionaries may provide some insight into this.[5] Whelchel conducted surveys of more than twenty-six hundred Southern Baptist missionaries, mapping out their personalities using the Meyers-Briggs Type Indicator (MBTI). He theorized that certain personality types would figure more prominently than others. He was most directly interested in the division between "extroversion" and "introversion." These terms describe how people gain (extroverts) or lose (introverts) energy when around other people.[6] According to Whelchel, three of the top five MBTI personality types favored extroversion.[7] In a later chapter, he made clear that the MBTI should not be used as a tool to predict success or failure in cross-cultural missions. He noted that a relationship between certain psychological characteristics "and continued missionary service was true for the missionaries in this study, but this fact should not be used as a determinative factor for others."[8]

Moreover, this idea is fascinating because it seems to venture into the realm of counterfactuals. In history and philosophy, counterfactuals ask how things might have been changed if a given historical event had either not taken place or happened differently than it did.[9] Sometimes the event in question is major; other times less so. In 2020-21, the National Geographic television channel showed commercials featuring important scientific figures such as Neil deGrasse Tyson and Jane Goodall. These persons were put in contexts different from those in which they made names for themselves: Tyson as a ride operator in an amusement park and Goodall as a reference librarian. The voice-over then asked, "What if the people who changed the world had never explored further?" Although a mild snobbery

---

5. Michael Eugene Whelchel, "The Relationship of Psychological Type to the Missionary Calling and Cross-Cultural Adjustment of Southern Baptist Missionaries" (DMiss diss., Asbury Theological Seminary, 1996), esp. 82-165.

6. Ibid., 104.

7. Ibid., 88.

8. Ibid., 231.

9. A series of historical questions like this are asked by the contributors to Niall Ferguson, ed., *Virtual History: Alternatives and Counterfactuals* (New York: Basic Books, 1997).

lies behind this question, the point remains valid. How important are the decisions that people make? Some decisions are more important than others, but only rarely does a particular decision make all the difference in the world.

Those who read the Bible in the context of a faith community can ask this kind of question about certain characters and the decisions they made. It is worth asking how things might have been different if Abraham[10] hadn't said yes to God. It seems clear that Abraham only went down in biblical history as a famous faithful follower of God because he did in fact say yes in Genesis 12. This is true even though his answer is not recorded verbally, the narrator simply telling us what Abraham did in response to God.

Let us ask this same question in two different ways. On the one hand, it seems easy to imagine Abraham not being the only one whom God asked to leave Ur. He was simply the first to say yes. On the other hand, it may be theologically problematic to think that God only has one person in mind who can accomplish a particular task. If God truly desires for all people to come to repentance (2 Pet. 3:9), it is difficult to imagine there only being one opportunity for any given person.

Generally speaking, a person should refrain from comparing herself and her life choices to a biblical character and that character's life choices. One way in which such a problematic comparison could be made is to suggest that for a person to truly follow God's call, she must do so in a dramatic way. This suggestion is mistaken. Not everyone who follows God does so in the same way or in the same or similar role. Both Old and New Testaments seem to bear this out. On the one hand, consider Amos,

---

10. Although he is called Abram in Genesis 12:1, he is better-known by the name Abraham, which God named him in 17:5. Much has been made in the past of the significance of this name change (e.g., from Abram, "exalted father," to Abraham, "father of a multitude"). However, the name change is irrelevant to the present essay, and the point seems strained anyway. Outside of the book of Genesis, the Old Testament only calls him Abram twice (1 Chron. 1:27; Neh. 9:7), with the Chronicler's genealogy simply equating the two names. Similarly, his wife Sarah is known as Sarai until Genesis 17:15.

who according to the book ascribed to him did not consider himself a likely prophet (Amos 7:14). Moreover, Jeremiah resisted God's call to be a prophet, calling himself unqualified, saying, "I do not know how to speak, for I am only a boy" (Jer. 1:6). Perhaps even Solomon may have grown up thinking he was unlikely to be king, since he was not the firstborn of his father David, even though his mother was perhaps already making some necessary political maneuvers.

In the New Testament, Paul suggests strongly that God calls people to a variety of different roles, so no one should think too highly of herself nor too lowly of someone else (1 Cor. 12). In addition, the writer of Ephesians 4 mentions that "some would be apostles, some prophets, some evangelists, some pastors and teachers, to equip the saints for ministry" (vv. 11-12). While all Christians, from a New Testament perspective, are called to follow the way of the cross, and following this way is not easy, individuals should not consider themselves more important or less important than other believers.

When God's call comes to someone, that person is probably not the only one who could do that job.

Many biblical characters could serve as evidence for this. The writer of Hebrews, along with highlighting the two biggest decisions of Abraham's life (Heb. 11:8-12, 17-19), discusses a large number of characters from the Old Testament. The writer seems almost to run out of breath trying to describe them all: "What else can I say? I do not even have enough time to tell you about Gideon, Samson, Barak, Jephthah, David and Samuel and the prophets—who through faithfulness conquered kingdoms, performed justice, obtained promises, shut the mouths of lions, extinguished the power of fire, escaped swords, getting strength out of weakness, becoming strong in warfare, making enemy camps run away" (vv. 32-34). These characters at the end of Hebrews 11 did many different things in response to God's call. This is why we can say that not everyone follows God in the same way. Indeed, it takes a special person to be an Abraham. Though someone else may have been able to do it, Abraham was the one who did.

When God's call comes to someone, that person is probably not the only one who could do that job. If a person doesn't like to do the work, God will find someone else. And God will find something else for that person to do. True enough, God gives us the ability to do what God wants us to do. We are not all called to do the same thing. However, God will not give up on us even if we prove to be too afraid or unwilling to do what God asks. The wider biblical tradition does affirm that God's people are, by and large, engaged in the same mission. The New Testament in particular, as noted, describes this mission using the very term "mission"—that is, the mission of God to reconcile the world to Godself (2 Cor. 5:19).

Other biblical characters also come to mind. Esther 4:12-14 suggests that God will deliver the Jews even if Esther doesn't help.[11] Also, in 1 Kings 19:4-18 God consoles Elijah that he is not in fact the only one who remains faithful to God. Some negative examples also present themselves. Even further back than the story of Abraham, one may ask, What if Adam and Eve had not taken the fruit from the tree? Thus it remains important to consider the intention of the author in crafting the narrative.

---

11. The problem is, rather, that Esther would not have been faithful to what God was telling her and that she received a warning of the consequences. Though at first appearance this aspect presents a challenge to our thesis, the challenge is easily met with two points. First, it is Mordecai who gives this warning, not God, who is completely (?) absent from the story. Second, and more important theologically, following God should not have guilt attached to it; rather, following "God's good, acceptable, and complete will" (Rom. 12:2) should be a matter of joy; Paul says that "God loves a cheerful giver" (2 Cor. 9:7).

Genesis 12:2: Good Is Better than Plenty

A short statement in Ecclesiastes 7:1 has, in the course of time, risen to the status of a cultural axiom: "A good name is better than fine oil." An alternative version comes in Proverbs 22:1, which reads, "A good name should be chosen over much wealth." In the Apocrypha, Sirach 41:13 is more expansive: "A good life lasts a certain number of days, but a good name continues forever." We noted above that Abraham's decision to follow God into unseen places was the first of two principal acts of faithfulness. In Genesis 12:2-3, God announces a series of blessings to follow on Abraham's first obedient act. The promise involves three things: (1) Abraham will be made into a great nation, (2) Abraham's name will be made great, and (3) Abraham will be a blessing. Verse 3, which we will deal with below, gives a little more explanation to the third of these promises. At the beginning of Abraham's story, he chooses the esteem that God promises instead of wealth. Ironically, Abraham was probably already quite wealthy even at this point in the narrative; verse 5 says as much. Wealthy or no, Abraham took a significant risk when he departed from the place where he had gathered all his possessions and set off in pursuit of the great reputation God offered him. As has already been shown, because of this faithful act, Abraham gains a great reputation.

Abraham's high reputation is secured in salvation history in spite of several apparent missteps along the way. Quite aside from the fact that it is problematic to look to biblical characters as something like comic-book superheroes of faithfulness and piety, faithful readers are forced to consider that Abraham did not always live up to this reputation in any case. First, he twice lied about his wife Sarah, saying that she was his sister. In the first instance, he asked Sarah to tell this to the Egyptian Pharaoh (v. 13). Second, he himself lied to a certain King Abimelech of a nation called Gerar (20:2). Historical-critical scholarship on Genesis has usually explained this doublet[12] by appealing to different complexes of tradition that were combined at some point in the history of the composition of Genesis. However, from a narrative standpoint, one can read these two episodes as reflecting something of the struggle Abraham faced. Though he still remains the father of faith, his reputation is tarnished in particular because of what these lies mean for Sarah: she is, in twenty-first-century language, trafficked into the harems of the two kings. She is only delivered after God attacks Egypt with plagues (surely a foreshadowing of Exodus) and threatens to do the same to Abimelech. The text remains silent on what Sarah may have thought about this situation, though one may certainly suppose that she was not pleased with it.

The second and third mistakes Abraham makes both come at the insistence of Sarah, though this does not lessen his responsibility. First, he accepts Sarah's offer to sleep with her maidservant Hagar, since they both believe that it may be through Hagar that Sarah will bear children. While this was an acceptable practice in the society that produced the story, theologically it represents a failure of trust on the part of both Abraham and Sarah. Moreover, once Hagar does have a son, she apparently takes a hostile tone toward Sarah. Oddly enough, this is the only time in the entire narrative in which anyone "curses" Abraham or Sarah. Genesis 12:3 warns that "anyone who curses you will be cursed." Sarah does attempt to curse Hagar and Ishmael by forcing Abraham to send them out of the family compound—a move which would likely result in their deaths. However, God turns the story around and cares for Hagar and Ishmael, even proclaiming through an angel that Hagar will herself become the ancestor of a great nation (16:10). One should note that Muslims trace their lineage to Abraham (Ibrahim) through Ishmael. Thus God took something that might well be considered a failure on the part of Abraham and Sarah and

---

12. A doublet is a repetition of an already encountered story or phrase. The term "doublet" is still used even if what is described occurs three or more times. In fact, Abraham and Sarah's son Isaac also passes his wife off as his sister, apparently to the same King Abimelech of Gerar, though he is called the king of the Philistines (Gen. 26:6-11).

turned it into a good thing. The Old Testament writers boldly describe the complete humanity of each character, including mistakes and failure. Philip Yancey states it well:

> The Bible's glimpses of our eternal state all indicate that what we endure on earth now, and how we respond, will inform that state, help bring it about, and be remembered there. Even the resurrected Jesus kept his scars.
>
> Redemption promises not replacement—a wholly new creation imposed on the old—but a transformation that somehow makes use of all that went before.[13]

Further on in the story, when Abraham dies, Ishmael and Isaac together bury him (25:9). In that verse, Isaac is mentioned first, even though he was not the firstborn, because he has the more prominent position. This is Israel's story, after all. A later text in the Jewish tradition, however, perhaps speaks to a continuing high regard for Ishmael. The *Midrash Tanḥuma* (tenth century CE) draws upon the second of Abraham's two great faithful acts as listed in Hebrews 11, the near-sacrifice of Isaac. This text imagines a dialogue between God and Abraham, while Genesis 22 records only the words of God:

> *And He said: "Take now (na) thy son, thine only son"* [Gen 22:2]. Abraham asked: "Which son is that?" The Holy One replied: *Your only son.* "But," he said, "one of my sons is the only son of his mother, and the other is the only son of his mother." *The son you love*, He replied. "I love them both," Abraham responded. "The one you love the most," said God. "Is there a limit in the viscera?" (i.e., Is there a measure within which a man gauges the love he bears his sons), he asked. Forthwith, God replied: *Isaac.*[14]

---

13. Philip Yancey, *Reaching for the Invisible God* (repr., Manila: OMF Literature, 2000), 255-56.

14. *Midrash Tanḥuma, Vayera* 22.2, trans. Samuel A. Berman, https://www.sefaria.org/Midrash_Tanchuma%2C_Vayera.22?lang=bi.

Abraham is not perfect in his responses to God's call, and so neither should anyone think they have to be. Moreover, Abraham's mistakes and their effects are not the final outcome; reconciliation always remains possible.

Genesis 12:3: God's Agent in and for the World

The series of blessings God promises to Abraham continues on into verse 3. Indeed, as we indicated in the previous section, the last verse gives a little more explanation to the third promise in verse 2: "I will bless you . . . so that you will be a blessing." In the Jewish tradition, the idea that Abraham was blessed to be a blessing formed the basis of a key theological idea about the people of Israel—namely, that they were God's chosen people. Deuteronomy 7:6-7 serves as a great example of this idea:

> For you are a people holy to the Holy One,[15] your God. The Holy One, your God, chose you out of all the peoples who are on the earth to be his prized people-possession. It was not because you had the biggest population of all the people that God loved you and chose you; in fact, you were the least among the peoples!

Why did God choose Israel to be God's chosen possession? Searching through Jewish literature, one can find a bewildering array of answers to this question. One answer is that the Israelites were chosen to help repair the world through their following of God's law. In much the same way as the New Testament and subsequent Christian theology worked out precisely what laws from the Old Testament needed to be incorporated into their situations, so also did postbiblical Judaism. Some of the rabbinical literature proposes, for example, that the covenant given to Moses applies to the Jews, while the covenant given to Noah and his sons applies

---

15. In this translation, I follow Wilda Gafney in the attempt to "translate the Divine Name reverently and contextually," without reference to a title commonly held by men. "Holy One," by contrast, is a term more often applied to God than to a human. See *Womanist Midrash: A Reintroduction to the Women of the Torah and the Throne* (Louisville, KY: Westminster John Knox Press, 2017), 286.

to all people. In light of all of this, we must bear in mind that Israel traced its lineage back to Abraham and Abraham's faithfulness to God. One of the reasons Abraham did what he did was because of God's promise that through him all of the families of the earth would be blessed.

This transforms following what God wants from being a chore or a burden to being something that has tremendous importance. Following the law is not a matter of trying to earn God's love (works righteousness), but instead it is a response to what God has done. One can see this in the Ten Commandments: all of those laws are based on God's prior action for the Israelites. This is also a key point in an authentic Wesleyan reading of Scripture. The New Testament bears witness to this as well, in particular in Romans 5:8 and 1 John 4:10, both of which emphasize God's prior movement of love toward humanity, even as God seeks human partners to advance the divine mission in the world.

According to this line of thinking, if Abraham and, by extension, the Israelites do what God is calling them to do, their obedience will have a lasting positive impact not only on them but also on the whole world. This idea calls forth a comparison with 2 Corinthians 5:18-19, mentioned above and quoted here in full: "All of this is from God, who reconciled us to himself through Christ and gave us the service of reconciliation. In other words, God was in Christ reconciling the world to himself, not counting their trespasses against them, having entrusted the message of reconciliation to us." Moreover, in Roman Catholic practice, so-called sacramentals are items meant to help people recall the benefit they receive from the sacraments of the church. For example, holy water helps people remember their baptism. The 1995 version of the Catholic catechism for the United States elaborates on this by saying, "Sacramentals derive from the baptismal priesthood: every baptized person is called to be a 'blessing,' and to bless."[16] The reference to Genesis 12:3 is interesting here: obedience to God on the part of the faithful has far-reaching effects. For Christians,

---

16. United States Catholic Conference, *Catechism of the Catholic Church: Complete and Updated* (Washington, DC: USCCB, 1995), 464.

these effects are not just about making people Christian, giving people a chance to respond positively to God's call in the gospel, though that is an important idea. Following God is about bringing the hope of a new orientation. We can work for real change in the world, in *this* world. Christians are called not just to prepare people for a new life in heaven but also to make life better for people who live here.

Conclusion

In this essay, we have explicated the biblical story of the call to Abraham to follow God to an unseen place. We began with the reminder that Judaism, Christianity, and Islam all trace their founding to this and the subsequent acts of obedience on Abraham's part. However, as we noted, the idea that Abraham was the only person whom God could possibly have called is theologically untenable. Though today Jews, Christians, and Muslims would not know the name of Abraham if he had not said yes to God, this surely does not justify a belief that his journey from Haran to Canaan could not have been taken by anyone else. Moreover, even granting that Abraham could have refused God's call, this does not mean that he would have been cast out of God's favor forever.

Following this, we took a deep look at the missteps that Abraham took along the way in his faithful journey. Some of his poor decisions led to terrible implications for others in his life, in particular Sarah, Hagar, and Ishmael. However, after he died, Ishmael and Isaac came together to bury him, indicating that perhaps these poor decisions and their effects were not the final word. Furthermore, we also briefly considered a Jewish text from the tenth century CE that appeared to highlight Abraham's equivalent concern for both of his sons.

Finally, we considered a very important theological concept: the identification of the Jews as God's chosen people. This idea has its origin in God's promise to make Abraham the source of blessing for all people. Though the meaning of this promise has many varied explanations throughout both Jewish and Christian history, one of the most important was the idea that God particularly chose the Jews to keep God's law, their faithfulness in that task contributing to healing the brokenness of the world. Finally, by exploring an application of "blessed to be a blessing" in Christian sacramental practice, we highlighted a deep connection between the two faiths.

Reflection

Genesis 12:1-3 emphasizes the broader Old Testament theme of the character and life of the covenant community (with God and each other). To explore this theme further, consider the following questions:

1. Have you ever had a perception that God might be calling you to do something unusual? How did you respond?

2. Have you ever felt as if you failed to do something God wanted you to do? Did you have a sense of guilt attached to this?

3. The stories of biblical characters often include their unwillingness to do something or their failure in it. How can reading these stories help us to avoid a sense of guilt or pressure in following God's call?

2
EXODUS 3:7
Michael G. VanZant

The LORD said, "I have indeed seen the misery of my people in Egypt.
I have heard them crying out because of their slave drivers,
and I am concerned about their suffering."
—Exodus 3:7

"Misery" is a word that breaks through the barriers of time and human existence. A broken world groans for a glimpse of hope, a taste of cool water, a sense of belonging in the darkness of despair. The cries of the Hebrews in Egyptian bondage resonate in just this way throughout Scripture and history. A desire for provision and the continuance of life, a place of belonging, and the embrace of community fill the hopes of all humans. Yet winds blowing in dry places often dash these hopes upon the rocks of disappointment, loss, and oppression of many types. At this intersection of human hope and despair, we find the story of Moses and the burning bush in Exodus 3:1-15.

Exodus 3:7 in the Old Testament

Throughout the biblical stories leading up to Exodus 3:1-15, God prepared Israel to survive various threats to the divine promise given to Abraham and Sarah (Gen. 12:1-3). Those threats included family dysfunction, famine, and enslavement. Joseph conveyed his father, Jacob, and his family to Egypt to escape the threat to life and place due to famine. They settled in the land of Goshen. Life prospered in this new place of belonging, blessed by Pharaoh's hospitality (Gen. 42–50). Still, this was not the land promised to Abraham, Isaac, and Jacob. Even in this time of prosperity, Jacob's multitude of descendants lived in a foreign land. In the immediate moment of happiness in a borrowed land, the threat of a Pharaoh "to whom Joseph meant nothing" (Exod. 1:8, NIV) lurked in the shadows.

In the first chapter of Exodus, the threat became real. The insecure, power-hungry Pharaoh killed Hebrew toddlers and babies (v. 22). Weeping and mourning of distraught parents echo throughout the story of Moses's salvation from the waters of the very Nile River meant to kill him (Exod. 2). Moses grew from miraculously preserved babe to murderer, fugitive, wanderer, husband, father, and, ultimately, a sojourner—a "foreigner in a foreign land" (2:22, NIV). A Hebrew, raised as an Egyptian, Moses then lived a desert dweller's life of sheepherding and wandering in the wilderness of Midian.

Back in Egypt, a land now far away from Moses, his Hebrew people suffered in slavery. Oppression and bondage increased to the breaking point! As readers, we sense the depths of groaning and the cries of people with no voice, for there was no one to listen to them. Just before our story at the burning bush, Exodus 2:23-25 allows the reader to imagine the rising, pitiful groans reaching up to God. And then God comes to meet Moses in the wilderness at the burning bush.

The Words

The verbs used in Exodus 3:7 are critical. God "heard" (Hebr., *shema'*), "has seen" (Hebr., *ra'ah*), and was "concerned" (Hebr., *yada'*). The intimate and relational nature of the verbs introduces the nature of God. Each of these words needs attention for the magnitude and mystery of Exodus 3:1-15 to move anew the senses of readers, perhaps especially those familiar with the story. Background noise and screaming voices affect the art of listening. Many voices bombard the senses of twenty-first-century people. Time to listen closely is hard to find. The Hebrew word *shema‘* carries the full weight of the idea "to hear." We hear with our ears, but not well. As my mother used to say, "What I told you went in one ear and out the other!" The human tendency to think of responses while someone still speaks taints true comprehension. The Hebrew term entails hearing with our ears, listening with our minds and hearts, owning what we hear, and responding to it rightly in thought, word, and deed.

God "sees" and calls us to see, with intention and attention.

The idea of "seeing" draws the reader to move beyond the glance, gaze, disinterested stare, or blank expression used and experienced often in life. God "sees" and calls us to see, with intention and attention. Nothing is wasted or lost due to an inattentive look. Details fill the mind through clear vision and true interest. When the cries and groans of hurting people rise, God does not give an annoyed glance wishing they would shut up! When a child's innocent prayers for her sick cat reach God's ears, God hears and looks with loving intent. This type of seeing requires action.

The Hebrew word *yada‘* literally means "to know." Often translated in terms of concern, care, and compassion, the word entails intimate knowledge. A desire to know and to be known deeply is the essence of relationship. The ability to know, see, and hear is a gift of God through the *imago Dei*, the image of God in humans. To know is to interact, understand, reason, and own what is learned. Once again, we see that knowledge requires action. To know is to care, love, and have compassion or passion concerning the "known."

With these verbs used by God at the beginning of the encounter with Moses, God's nature revealed through images and allusions in Genesis become alive in the words from God's own thoughts. God is personal. God is compassionate. God is present. In the story of the burning bush, God's thoughts become living words spoken into a relationship that will change the course of Israel's history. A homeless and oppressed people, the promise of life threatened by oppression, a fugitive with a muddled identity wandering in the wilderness, and a God who hears, sees, and knows make for amazing drama!

Presence in Action: God, Moses, and the Burning Bush

Reading Exodus 3:1-15 as merely an entertaining story makes a mockery of its intent. The events detailed in the text describe no ordinary day in a shepherd's life. The style and type of writing reveal an extraordinary experience that is timeless in importance within Israel's history and for the church. The infinite breaks into the finite. God enters history to bring redemption and release from captivity through a shepherd leathered by the sun and by life's experiences. An intentional God meets a reluctant servant for the purpose of doing what seems impossible. Moses speaks for every human with his words, "Who am I?" (v. 11, NIV). God's response continues to unfold through human history: "I AM is with you" (v. 14).

Exodus 3:1

After the interlude in 2:23-25, the story returns to Moses after many years of life in Midian. His father-in-law's name has changed from Reuel (v. 18) to Jethro (3:1). Moses is still a shepherd seeking new grazing land "behind" (or most likely "deep into") the wilderness near Mount Horeb, another name for Mount Sinai. "Horeb" carries the idea of "Parched Mountain." Ironically, Moses's story that began on the lush shores of the Nile River now finds him a long way from Goshen and in the parched and dusty wilderness. The man raised as a child in a busy palace and rich lands is now an old man alone with his flock in a lonely desert place, unaware that he is about to meet God face-to-face.

What went through his mind during the long, cold nights and the hot, dry days in the wilderness? Did the oppression of his people that resulted in his fugitive status cross his mind in that wilderness? The verse concludes with promise, unknown to Moses, as he "came to Horeb, the mountain of God" (NIV). Moses's wanderings led him to a divine appointment. Whether previously known as a sacred mountain or only recognized in hindsight, the final phrase of the verse awakens our senses with anticipation!

Exodus 3:2-3

Theophany, a visible manifestation of God, expresses God's transcendence and yet also reveals God's immanence and desire for relationship. Although God is distinct from the world, throughout Scripture God is revealed in ways identifiable to humans. God "comes down" in theophany to Moses for the purpose of redemption. A key aspect of this theophany is the media used. The Lord's messenger appears in the midst of a bush mysteriously aflame yet not consumed. Who is the messenger whose presence appears out of nowhere? Was the messenger's purpose to produce the flames through which the Lord speaks? Regardless, the intent of the phenomenon was to attract Moses's attention.

Success follows quickly. Moses notices with amazement that the bush burns but is not consumed. Moses "sees" and is compelled to act: "Moses said, I will turn aside, now, and see this great sight why this bush does not burn up" (v. 3). The word translated "now" is an interjection that is also rendered, "I pray." The sense of urgency and immediacy is important to the text. He must go! Moses immediately moves toward the mountainside experience that will challenge his senses and courage in ways inconceivable to him or any initial readers of the story. Upon his arrival, the bush and fire lose all mention in the story. Moses comes into the active presence of God. The messenger's work is complete. The voice of God takes over.

The God of the patriarchs and matriarchs in Genesis, who called Abraham and Sarah, who fulfilled promises by opening the wombs of barrenness, who "goes with" those called, who protected and kept the promise through imperfect humans throughout Genesis, now speaks to the fugitive murderer with one intent: to show that God is faithful to promises made. God's promise to Abraham and Sarah was expansive: "And your family will be a blessing to all the families of the earth" (Gen. 12:3). The blessing to "all" the world through Abraham's descendants, however, now faces extinction in exile from the land of promise. The voice of one calling in the wilderness prepares the way for the long journey to fulfillment of this promise through Jesus Christ.

Exodus 3:4-6

Often lost in the familiarity of the story is the remarkable fact that God knew Moses by name. The double statement of Moses's name here recalls another critical moment of threat to the promise in Genesis 22:11. As Abraham's hand held the knife high in the air, prepared to sacrifice his promised son, the call from heaven came. In both stories, the response "Here I am" rings with hope (NIV). God's voice declares attention, care, concern, and presence that reveal the nature of God's tender, loving mercy. Human response to God's presence breathes life into the promise of salvation.

God's presence preempts the normal and transforms dust, sand, rock, and a scrubby bush into sacred ground. Key to this encounter is the reality of God's awesome holiness in separation, demanding respectful distance. The conversation is at God's initiative and intention. Submission is required in the act of baring the feet while on holy ground. The wilderness is transformed into a temple of worship, and the divine presence moves Moses to hide his face and eyes. Moses finds himself laid bare before the great and dreadful holiness of God. Wonder fills the moment and continues to do so in the hearts of careful readers. Anticipation fills the wind that blows through the wilderness and through the hearts of captive, oppressed, and despised people in need of liberation and justice.

God says, "I am the God of your father, the God of Abraham, the God of Isaac and the God of Jacob" (Exod. 3:6, NIV). The present tense of the entire statement foreshadows the revelation of God's name later in the passage. This formulaic statement appears throughout Israel's story, as even the Psalms and Prophets recount God's saving acts.

Exodus 3:7-10

God is. Therefore, God sees the oppression and abuse of the children of Jacob, "my people" (v. 7, NIV). Incredibly, God sees their outcry from Egypt. Remember the verbs used in verse 7! The pain of fearful people and tormented bodies is seen and known, not just heard from far off. God knows their pain and circumstances with an intimacy that drives compassionate action from God's nature. Active hearing embraces those speaking with all the senses and requires action on the hearer's part.

God hears and cares for all who cry out
in oppression and injustice.

Neither this section nor the "prelude" of Exodus 2:23-25 specifically say that the outcries of the oppressed were "prayers" to God. They are the deep, heartfelt cries of the oppressed, the moans of the crushed in spirit, and the only expression of hope mustered in the middle of hopelessness. Their cries reflect the image of God in humans who know deep in their beings that oppression and abuse are not how things should be. The love and justice of God's nature spark humans in the hands of systemic evil to groan and cry out through and against injustice. In many ways, groans and cries, crying out against abusive treatment, are the impetus of hope and survival. The belief that someone will hear, see, care, and save keeps the oppressed alive in the struggle.

The fact that God hears the cries of the oppressed, even when they are not specific addresses to God as prayers, exposes an important truth. God hears and cares for all who cry out in oppression and injustice. Systemic evil is never a "necessary" evil in God's economy of creation. Fallen humanity's treatment of each other exposes the redemptive need within all of creation, which groans with anticipation for salvation (Rom. 8:21-22).

The active presence of God calls humans to deliver the oppressed, whose plight and cries reach divine eyes and ears. The prophets cry out for justice for the poor whose heads are crushed and the needy who are oppressed (Amos 4:1). The Egyptians abused the Hebrews for their profit and feared the Hebrews' numbers. Self-interest and a desire for control lead people to oppress, allow oppression, or ignore oppression of the other. This story calls for a different response. The question "Who am I?" (the question Moses will soon ask) must be considered by all who read this passage.

Verse 8 notes that God "comes down" to "raise up, bring up" the oppressed into a good land. The word "good" is often misunderstood in common vernacular. "Good" may mean average, so-so, not quite better or best. Yet a full view of the Hebrew word here reveals a scope that is missing in common English. "Good" carries the idea of having everything necessary for life. God finished creation and declared that it was very good, completed. Good does not mean perfect. Good creation can be developed and improved but is to be tended and cared for, not abused and oppressed.

Further, the self-revealing nature of God's activity overshadows the entire story. The active presence of the infinite invades the finite. God is not compelled to act due to human worth or goodness. Human manipulation by acts of religious ritual does not motivate God's action. Deliverance is a free gift provided by God's nature of divine love and mercy. In this story, God had the freedom to do or not do. But God sees, hears, knows and cares, and comes down to deliver out of bondage because of the "Is-ness" of Being that humans find difficult to describe adequately.

The description of the land and its current inhabitants in Exodus 3:8 provides a glimpse of provision and deliverance within the story. God comes down to bring up the oppressed from the land of death and hopelessness (Egypt) and deliver them to a land of life and promise (Canaan). Deliverance includes a place of belonging, the hope of continued life, and the promise of community. Deliverance is not a "get out of hell (Egypt) free" card. It is a call to wholeness of life that promotes continued growth within a relationship with the deliverer and others. Deliverance demands acceptance of responsibility to reciprocate mercy shown, nurturing the place provided to allow life to flourish for all who need hope and responding to the deliverer's tender, loving mercy with love for God and others. Exodus 3:7-9, in fulfillment of 2:24-25, reveals that God alone is the only hope of salvation for Israel and for all humans lost in the land of death.

Exodus 3:8 is one of those places where the old children's game of Chutes and Ladders is helpful. Reading all of the "-ites" in the land may cause English speakers to stumble. We are tempted to slide right past them to get to the "good stuff." Yet the full context of the section reveals a sense of a quickening tenor through the relating of each name. We sense God hurrying through the list. For "now, look," the cries and oppression of the people fill God's senses (v. 9). The time for action and deliverance is now! God's tender, loving mercy is freely given and unearned. Salvation draweth nigh!

If only verse 10 could be ignored! With a sudden twist, the issue of human choice to participate in God's act of deliverance takes center stage. Moses is the one on the spot. We can imagine Moses's thoughts when he hears, "Now, go!" He might think, "Yeah, but God, you were the one who saw, who heard, who cares, and who comes down to deliver, so you go!" His mind likely went through the possibilities of success or death. Moses knew the power of Pharaoh whose single word could bring death. He was a fugitive wanted for murder in Egypt. The Israelites were a major cog in the economic and power structure of Pharaoh's success. The whole episode would be difficult even with a mighty army behind him and, rightly, seems impossible for a single shepherd-wanderer, refugee, fugitive, and foreigner in a foreign land. The task is impossible to achieve on human terms!

God's move into human history is odd compared to stories of other cultures in which domineering gods toy with humans for fun. God's work is for the good of creation. God's presence is in relationship with the created, not demanding power and control, but working through weak and vulnerable humans.

Exodus 3:11

"Who am I?" (v. 11, NIV). This is a logical question in response to an illogical request. This expression of unworthiness is admirable but also fails to account for the setting in which Moses finds himself. Yes, Moses, who are you to question the great God of the universe? Who are you to see the power of God before you, hear the voice of God directly, know firsthand that everything God spoke was truth, and yet question?

Moses is all of us. "But, God, wait a minute. I am no speaker." "I cannot sing." "I can't go to Africa. . . . I've got these sheep and children." "Don't you know that my neighbor is mean?" "Those people hate us!" "Who am I?" usually means, "I don't want to!" Moses confronts us regularly. Thank God for grace and mercy and for the rest of the story. Moses will deliver the people from Egypt, yet not alone.

Exodus 3:12

God does not call someone to undertake a mission in difficult circumstances only to flounder in ineptitude. God does not set anyone up for failure. God says, "I will be with you" (v. 12, NIV). The implications and possibilities wrapped in this statement are unfathomable! The promise of divine presence, an active presence, is beyond human comprehension. Even this story provides no explanation of how this presence works. But God is with us! This is another statement that all too often loses its powerful impact through familiarity to the readers of Scripture. The idea of the eternal, infinite Spirit of God being present within time and place must remain a glorious mystery. Heaven and earth meet in the willing though often fearful heart. Amazement is certain in response to this marvelous declaration of the creator of the universe, "I am with you!"

Knowing Moses's doubts and weaknesses, the sign that God provides is unique in its promise and requirement of faith. Moses will see the sign of promise only after the task is complete. Mount Horeb, the parched mountain, becomes the sign of promise. Once Moses's quest to Egypt begins, God's presence will appear through signs and wonders, plagues, cloud, and fire. Yet only when Moses returns to the mountain of conversation will God's voice be heard once more. Between the mountain visits, divine presence is a matter of faith in the difficulties, rejections, and successes.

Verse 12 contains an interesting verb concerning Moses's return to "this mountain" (NIV). Moses will not return to celebrate his victories. Moses will return to the mountain to "serve" (Hebr., 'avad) the Lord. In this context, "to serve" includes worship and reverence. Yet the term reveals a continuation of the call and the responsibility of being a servant of God. The return to Horeb (Sinai) will not be a "look what I/we did" moment but a look toward the "what's next" of faithful walking. The promise of presence empowers weak humans to do amazing things, no matter how small, in a lifetime of service on mountains or in valleys.

Exodus 3:13-15

Still Moses is uncertain and unsure of the results of the mission. God's promise of presence is great, but "Who are you, God?" To this point, the God of Abraham, Isaac, and Jacob was given names by humans that reveal God's active presence in various situations: El-roi (God Sees), Jehovah-jireh (The "LORD" [YHWH] Provides), El-Shaddai (God Most High). These and many other names attempt to articulate human understanding of the living God who is present and active.

In verses 13-15, Moses's second issue of reluctance remains deeply rooted in the human psyche. The full mystery of who God is remains a challenge to understand. For Moses and his people in bondage, the issue is more straightforward: "Who will save us?" Names in the ancient world were descriptive. Most Hebrew names translate into an action or status. The name of the deliverer would reveal the nature of this one who was issuing a call and a promise to Moses. Before people trust someone, they often want to know who he or she is and what motives he or she possesses. So, Moses inquires, "If they ask me, 'Who is this God,' what do I tell them?" While often seen as a lack of faith, the question is logical and perceptive. The answer will provide two important points of information. First, what kind of God is the Lord? Is this a fertility god, a warrior god, or any other of the plethora of gods in the ancient world? Second, what is the nature of this God's rule? Many ancient gods were thought to rule only in certain locations within nations or cities. This idea remained in Israel's thinking until the exile. God's presence residing in the temple of Jerusalem brought false hope to Judah during the Babylonian crises. Moses had heard God say that they would speak again on "this mountain." Is this a wilderness God? Much of Israel's historical remembrance of God in the rest of Scripture is of the wilderness. Within the question may be a hint of concern: Will God's presence be with Moses in Egypt?

The revelation of God's name in these verses proclaims presence, faithfulness, integrity, and power: "I AM WHO I AM" (v. 14, NIV). The name indicates one whose being and presence extend through all time: "I Will Be Who I Will Be," "I Am That I Am," "I Am the One Who Endures." These are but a few of the attempts to translate this name.

How do we explain the name of God as "I Am"? In the rest of the Old Testament, the divine name becomes formulated in Hebrew as *YHWH*, translated as "the LORD" in English translations. Most likely, the term is related to a Hebrew verb form meaning "One Who Brings Things into Existence." Several implications from this name are clear: God is. God causes all things to exist. God is the one who has power to bring life into being. God is present and trustworthy. God is continually "new" and brings "newness" from decay.

The divine name is not fully knowable and impossible to decipher in human terms. Yet our passage links the name with God's acts in Genesis. "The LORD" was present with Abraham, Isaac, Jacob, and their families. The "Giver of Life" opened the wombs of Sarah, Rebekah, and Rachel. Joseph knew God's presence, albeit often in hidden ways, so that he could save the lives of his family, as well as the lives of all people during a famine. "I Am" heard the cries, saw the tears, knew the suffering, and came to deliver an oppressed people.

Our passage ends with a simple statement, "This is my name forever, the name you shall call me from generation to generation" (v. 15, NIV). Remember this day for all generations. Teach your children the meaning of this name. Remind them of the God of their ancestors who continues to hear, see, know, and deliver. "I am with you" means "I was, am, and will always be" with the crushed in spirit, the oppressed, and the lost in search of a home.

Conclusion

The church finds its roots within the Old Testament traditions through Jesus Christ, the "I Am." The Gospel of John connects the "Word" in its opening verses with Jesus, who identifies himself as "I am" in seven statements throughout the book. Acts 2 boldly declares the power of divine presence in the gift of the Holy Spirit. Revelation 1:8 identifies God as the Alpha and Omega, "the one who is, was, and is to come"—in that order! The incredible, present "Is-ness" of an infinite God continues to manifest itself in an active, personal presence. God still calls weak and frail human beings to be agents of deliverance and good news. God still sees, hears, knows, cares deeply, and comes to deliver!

Reflection

Exodus 3:1-15 expresses the broader Old Testament themes of God's saving work (especially through deliverance of the oppressed) and God's ongoing presence in the covenant community as it participates in God's acts of deliverance for others. Consider some of these practices and questions concerning God's delivering work and guiding presence today:

1. Think of an occasion when you may have been like Moses in your reluctance to "go" in response to God's calling. Why? Forgive yourself. Even Moses was reluctant. Grab hold of the promise "I am with you," and consider what is next.

2. Write a statement of faith for each of these key words: "see," "hear," and "know." What does it mean for God to do these things? How can you practice these things, especially toward the most vulnerable in your community?

3
EXODUS 19:5
Jennifer M. Matheny

> *Now, therefore, if you obey my voice and keep my covenant,*
> *you shall be my treasured possession out of all the peoples.*
> —Exodus 19:5a, NRSV

Exodus 19:5 in the Old Testament

"'The Eagles! The Eagles!' he shouted. 'The Eagles are coming!'"[1] In moments of hopelessness throughout J. R. R. Tolkien's book *The Hobbit*, eagles play a significant and salvific role. In this quote from chapter 17, Bilbo Baggins is excited to see the descent of the eagles, knowing from previous experience that the presence of eagles represents rescue and hope in perilous times. In the darkest moments, aid comes from the heavens above, as these majestic birds swoop down to rescue, bringing them *up* and *out* to safety. In *The Hobbit*, eagles represent life.

Exodus 19:1-6 reveals a key moment that describes Israel's redemption from slavery to a vocation of holiness, life, and blessing. This calling is carried throughout the entire Old Testament. From its inception through exile and beyond, Israel will retain its identity as a chosen people whose

---

1. J. R .R. Tolkien, *The Hobbit, or There and Back Again* (New York: Random House, 1982), 124.

role is to mediate God's plan of blessing for the world. Israel's identity is formed through this story of God's rescue, how the Lord carried them from death to life, on *eagle's wings*. Exodus 19:1-6 describes the mighty salvific acts of God:

> Three months after leaving Egypt the Israelites entered the Wilderness of Sinai. They followed the route from Rephidim, arrived at the Wilderness of Sinai, and set up camp. Israel camped there facing the mountain.
>
> As Moses went up to meet God, God called down to him from the mountain: "Speak to the House of Jacob, tell the People of Israel: 'You have seen what I did to Egypt and how I carried you on eagles' wings and brought you to me. If you will listen obediently to what I say and keep my covenant, out of all peoples you'll be my special treasure. The whole Earth is mine to choose from, but you're special: a kingdom of priests, a holy nation.'
>
> "This is what I want you to tell the People of Israel." (MSG)

The metaphor of the eagle, which describes God's rescue, shapes Israel's story in significant ways. This story of God's redemptive acts in Exodus is the foundation of Israel's covenant commitment. It is the preamble of rescue to the Ten Commandments (literally, "ten words"): "I am the LORD your God, who brought you out of Egypt, out of the land of slavery" (20:2, NIV).

This rescue story is where Israel, as a people, learns to trust God in the wilderness. Israel is called to be a holy people. This call centers on relational holiness with God and one another, a relationship rooted in the *hesed* (Hebr., "faithful love") of God. Exodus 19:1-6 is a key text that reveals that God is not only the rescuer of the oppressed but also one who transforms Israel through their corporate calling and invites them into the sacred task of participating as a holy and chosen people in order to bless the world. The Lord promises to be with Israel and to help form Israel in this calling. They will not be left alone to figure this out. In fact, the image of an eagle with her young resurfaces in Deuteronomy 32:10-11 in the song of Moses. This image describes the Lord as a mother eagle:

> In a desert land he found him,

in a barren and howling waste.
He shielded him and cared for him;
he guarded him as the apple of his eye,
like an eagle that stirs up its nest
and hovers over its young,
that spreads its wings to catch them
and carries them aloft. (NIV)

The events in Exodus reveal a story of salvation that becomes a pattern retold, reimagined, and reinterpreted throughout the Old and New Testaments. During the transfiguration (another mountaintop moment), Moses and Elijah discuss with Jesus his exodus that would soon take place in Jerusalem (Luke 9:30-31). The Gospels reflect back on the movements of God in Exodus to illustrate the work of Christ. Even the church is viewed through the exodus motif, and exodus becomes the vocabulary through which the biblical writers share the stories of God's saving work of redemption, deliverance, covenant, and divine presence.

The Context of Sinai: Creation, Divine Presence, Deliverance, Creation, Covenant

An acronym from the urban dictionary helpfully frames the significant moment between the Lord and Israel at Sinai in Exodus 19:1-6: DTR. This acronym stands for *define the relationship.*

When I was visiting Westmont College (Santa Barbara, California) on a campus tour with my daughter, Emma, our tour guide directed us to the "DTR spot" on campus, which was next to a beautiful pond. Here couples would sit on the bench together and have "the talk." I imagine many of us recall similar moments when friendships crossed over into romantic, committed relationships, with our hearts all aflutter! Here at Sinai, the Lord has wooed Israel through mighty acts of deliverance and provision. The Lord shares with Israel that they are unique, that they have a special status, and invites them to respond with a covenant proposal. In some ways, Sinai is the most epic DTR moment in the entire Old Testament!

Understanding Exodus 19:1-6 within the larger context of the Old Testament reveals why it is one of the twelve passages chosen for this volume.

Not only is Exodus 19:1-6 a mountaintop moment in the story of the Old Testament, but it also takes place at "the mountain of God." Other terms used for this place are Mount Horeb (3:1-12; Deut. 4:10) and Mount Sinai (Exod. 19–24; Deut. 33:2). More significant than location or name is what this place represents for the people of Israel.[2] This mountain is a destination point after their dramatic deliverance through the Reed Sea and the wilderness wanderings and will be a place in their memory that marks their identity and vocation as a chosen and holy people. This people, with a holy calling, are now created and formed as a new community. Exodus 19:1-6 marks the moment; it defines the relationship. This destination spot is *a* destination but not the *final* destination. In fact, Sinai in the Old Testament was not a pilgrimage destination. Mount Sinai functions in their memory as a sacred place in their rhetoric of liturgy. What happens on this mountain illustrates a high point in identity, calling, and creation as a covenant *people*. Israel learns that their status as a chosen people predates their covenant commitment. In fact, "the covenant concept is the dominant metaphor in the Hebrew Bible for the relationship between God and the Israelites."[3] Covenant (*berit*) represents a relational contract, similar to those in ancient Western Asia (such as the suzerainty treaty or vassal treaty).[4] Through this covenant, Israel will learn that their unique role and calling reveals God's divine presence in the world and God's love for all of creation.

---

2. The location of Mount Sinai is often associated with the mountain on the Sinai Peninsula located in Egypt, but biblical scholars are not certain of its exact geographic location. Exodus 19:11 is the first time the phrase "Mount Sinai" is found.

3. Carol Meyers, *Exodus*, New Cambridge Bible Commentary (Cambridge, UK: Cambridge University Press, 2005), 148.

4. Similarities in the covenant format can be seen with the Hittite treaties from the second millennium BCE. This reveals that the covenant contract was a familiar legal form in this context, and yet the relationship between Yhwh and Israel is unique.

The story of Exodus not only is a pivotal moment in the Old Testament but also comprises specific lexical and thematic connections to creation language in Genesis. It is clear that Exodus is continuing the story of Genesis, because it starts with the conjunction "and" (similar to Leviticus and Numbers). Often we think of Old Testament books as separate, yet this conjunction reminds us that these stories are meant to be read together. Along with the conjunction, there is also the shared language of creation and covenant in Genesis and Exodus. This language of creation and covenant illustrate the links between these two books.

Table 3.1. Language of Creation and Covenant[5]

Gen. 2:1	Exod. 39:32
Thus the heavens and the earth were *completed* in all their vast array. (Emphasis added)	So all the work on the tabernacle, the tent of meeting, was *completed*. The Israelites did everything just as the LORD commanded Moses. (Emphasis added)
Gen. 1:28*a*	**Exod. 1:6-7**
God blessed them and said to them, "Be *fruitful* and *increase in number*; fill the earth and subdue it." (Emphasis added)	Now Joseph and all his brothers and all that generation died, but the Israelites were exceedingly *fruitful*; they multiplied greatly, *increased in numbers* and became so numerous that the land was filled with them. (Emphasis added)
Gen. 1:31; 2:3*a*	**Exod. 39:43**
God *saw* all that he had made . . . . . . [and] *blessed* the seventh day. (Emphasis added)	Moses inspected the work and *saw* that they had done it just as the LORD had commanded. So Moses *blessed* them. (Emphasis added)

---

5. Scripture quotations in table 3.1 are from the NIV.

Gen. 2:3	Exod. 40:9
Then God blessed the seventh day and *made it holy*, because on it he rested from all the work of creating that he had done. (Emphasis added)	Take the anointing oil and anoint the tabernacle and everything in it; consecrate it and all its furnishings, and it *will be holy*. (Emphasis added)
Gen. 2:2	**Exod. 31:12-17 (See also 16:1-23; 31:12-17; 35:1-3)**
By the seventh day God had finished the work he had been doing; so on the seventh day he *rested from* all his work. (Emphasis added)	Then the LORD said to Moses, "Say to the Israelites, 'You must observe my Sabbaths. This will be a sign between me and you for the generations to come, so you may know that I am the LORD, who makes you holy.
	"'Observe the Sabbath, because it is holy to you. Anyone who desecrates it is to be put to death; those who do any work on that day must be cut off from their people. For six days work is to be done, but the seventh day is a day of *sabbath rest*, holy to the LORD. Whoever does any work on the Sabbath day is to be put to death. The Israelites are to observe the Sabbath, celebrating it for the generations to come as a lasting covenant. It will be a sign between me and the Israelites forever, for in six days the LORD made the heavens and the earth, and on the seventh day he rested and was refreshed.'" (Emphasis added)

In table 3.1, themes from Genesis, such as God's presence, weave throughout the story and accompany God's people throughout Exodus. Divine presence is captured through anthropomorphic language. Anthropomorphic language describes God in terms that relate to humanity, terms such as *seeing, hearing, walking,* and *feeling.* In Exodus 2:24-25, God "sees," "hears," and "remembers." When Israel cries out, God responds to save them and "brings them up" from under the oppressive hand of Pharaoh and "brings them out" to worship God on the mountain, likened to a rescue on eagles' wings! Even after the incredible rescue, when Israel later complains and grumbles (16:2) in the wilderness, God listens to them. Rather than responding in anger, God provides bread and quail for them. These gifts provide substance, while the instructions for gathering the bread—providing weekly rhythms of work and Sabbath rest—train them to trust God and one another (vv. 1-18).

Covenant language also continues from the Genesis story into Exodus. The opening scene in Exodus paints a distressing portrait for the enslaved people of Israel. Once living under the blessings of Egypt, the story has now turned to a lamentable state of affairs. One of the critical factors in Israel's painful situation as Exodus opens is that the new Pharaoh does not remember Joseph (1:8). The leader of the country has forgotten. Has God forgotten Israel too? As the story unfolds, the covenant promise to Abraham will be reiterated and reintroduced to Moses and then through Moses to all of Israel. Not only does God remember this covenant promise, but God is also about to include the entire nation of Israel in a covenant relationship in order to mediate God's blessing to the world! In moments where Israel may have felt alone, God continues to be present in unexpected ways. God hears Israel's cries and responds. God delivers, God provides, and God enters into a covenant with Israel.

The Sinai mountaintop moment in Exodus 19:1-6 is a defining moment that can be traced from another significant moment in Genesis. Goldingay reminds us of the sacrifice of the initial covenant call to Abraham. Abraham was asked to give up country, homeland, and even family. This call is "devastating in its negativity."[6] Despite the sacrifice, Abraham says yes to the invitation to walk with God, to be a blessing to the nations, and to be blameless (Gen. 12:3; 17:1; 18:18). From a small family in Gene-

---

6. John Goldingay, *Genesis*, Baker Commentary on the Old Testament Pentateuch (Grand Rapids: Baker Academic, 2020), 207.

sis, Israel has grown to a nation in Exodus! This earlier covenant language anticipates God's call to Moses (Exod. 3:5) and the invitation to Israel to be a holy nation (19:6).

Mount Horeb (later called Mount Sinai), the "mountain of God," will be the place where Moses will be invited to lead Israel out of Egypt. This moment is described as a *theophany*.[7] In this moment, Moses will be reminded of his identity. Moses straddles two worlds, as a Hebrew boy raised in a wealthy and powerful Egyptian family and later as a refugee in Midian and married to a Midianite woman, Zipporah (2:15). Questions of identity and belonging surely cross Moses's mind. Which people is he part of? Where does Moses *belong*? The meaning of the name of their firstborn son, Gershom, reveals this anxious disposition: "I have become a foreigner in a foreign land" (v. 22, NIV). The Lord reminds Moses that his identity is rooted in the Abrahamic covenant promise. During the theophany on Horeb, the mountain of God, the Lord says to Moses, "I am the God of your father, the God of Abraham, the God of Isaac and the God of Jacob" (3:6, NIV). Whatever complexities of identity exist within Moses's inner dialogue, these words tell Moses that his call and lineage is connected to the covenant people (Gen. 15, 17).

Along with Moses, the people of Israel will learn that their movement from bondage to freedom will now entail an identity and calling beyond anything they could have imagined. Exodus 19:1-6 reveals that this covenant promise extends to all of Israel (chs. 19–24). Israel will now be invited to participate in God's redemptive ways in the world. The movement from Genesis to Exodus begins with a chosen family and will now extend to and through the entire people of God: Israel.

---

7. See chapter 2 in this volume by Michael G. VanZant, "Exodus 3:7."

The Calling: A Treasured Possession, a Holy Nation, and a Kingdom of Priests

Exodus 19:1-6 reveals that God is one who not only delivers Israel but also desires relationship. The covenant at Mount Sinai focuses on relationship and worship. This moment on the mountain has been anticipated since Exodus 3:11-12: "But Moses said to God, 'Who am I that I should go to Pharaoh and bring the children of Israel out of Egypt?' He said, 'But I will be with you, and this shall be the sign for you, that I have sent you: when you have brought the people out of Egypt, you shall serve God on this mountain'" (ESV). After the exodus, Israel journeys through the desert for three months and finally arrives at Mount Sinai, the mountain of God! God's divine presence will continue to be with them. Here they will be invited into a covenant with the Lord. Israel will be given this invitation in Exodus 19:1-6. Exodus 19–24 details the relationship with YHWH and within community. Exodus 25–40 will instruct the people of Israel on the practice of worship in their ancient context. At Mount Sinai, they will be formed in this place as God's people.

This covenant relationship is an invitation to participate in God's holy ways in the world, to become part of God's story. This invitation is connected to identity and calling. In order to be transformed as a holy people, Israel will be invited to respond: "Now if you obey me fully and keep my covenant, then out of all nations you will be my treasured possession. Although the whole earth is mine, you will be for me a kingdom of priests and a holy nation" (19:5-6, NIV). This invitation reveals that Israel is not coerced into this calling but is freely invited to respond. This calling begins with the Israelites' identity and formation as mediators of blessing. In order to live out this calling, Israel will be shaped through torah obedience, learning God's ways in the world. The people will learn how to love, to be merciful, and to be just. This is the way of holiness (Lev. 19:2). Law permeates the very fabric of life. Before the Israelites will say yes to this covenant relationship, God reminds them of their status as a treasured possession, a holy nation, and a kingdom of priests. "The way to be this kind of people is to keep the covenant; to keep the covenant is to be this kind of people."[8]

In this covenant proposal, the Lord calls Israel "my treasured possession." The Hebrew term for this phrase is *segullah* and can be understood as "treasured possession," "special possession," or "possession." It is found eight times in the Old Testament. Two relate to the idea of personal property as it refers to the king's assets (1 Chron. 29:3; Eccles. 2:8), but the majority of the occurrences indicate a symbolic understanding as we have here in Exodus 19:5.

Table 3.2. *Segullah* as "Treasured Possession"[9]

Exod. 19:5
Now if you obey me fully and keep my covenant, then out of all nations you will be my *treasured possession*. (Emphasis added)
Deut. 7:6
For you are a people holy to the LORD your God. The LORD your God has chosen you out of all the peoples on the face of the earth to be his people, his *treasured possession*. (Emphasis added)
Deut. 14:2
For you are a people holy to the LORD your God. Out of all the peoples on the face of the earth, the LORD has chosen you to be his *treasured possession*. (Emphasis added)
Deut. 26:18
And the LORD has declared this day that you are his people, his *treasured possession* as he promised, and that you are to keep all his commands. (Emphasis added)
Ps. 135:4
For the LORD has chosen Jacob to be his own, Israel to be his *treasured possession*. (Emphasis added)

---

8. Terence E. Fretheim, *Exodus,* Interpretation (Louisville, KY: John Knox Press, 1991), 213.

9. Scripture quotations in table 3.2 are from the NIV.

> **Mal. 3:17**
>
> "On the day when I act," says the LORD Almighty, "they will be my *treasured possession*. I will spare them, just as a father has compassion and spares his son who serves him." (Emphasis added)

The term *segullah* carries the idea of being carefully selected and tended, a chosen people with a *purpose*. Just as YHWH chose Jacob, YHWH has also chosen Jacob's descendants, the nation of Israel (Ps. 135:4). As YHWH's *segullah*, Israel's role is to be holy *and* to serve as mediators of God's plans and purposes.

Within the Old Testament, Israel is given the status as a holy nation. Holiness is an important concept throughout Exodus. Sometimes it is associated with specific items (such as sacrifices or clothing), and at other times it defines boundaries around sacred space with the construction of the tabernacle (e.g., holy of holies). In this moment in Exodus 19:5, holiness describes a people. This holy community would be set apart *from* the other nations *for* the purpose of worshipping YHWH only. They were to live dedicated lives to God in a world that belongs to God ("all the earth is mine" [Exod. 19:5*b*, ESV]). God's view is creation-wide in its scope. Within the Old Testament, Israel is chosen out of the world to be a holy nation and a kingdom of priests for the sake of the world. Israel's special status as the Lord's "firstborn" (Exod. 4:23, NIV) involves formation through trusting the Lord. Becoming a *holy* nation involves continued obedience, listening to the Lord, and keeping covenant. This is who they are *to be*. Again, Israel is invited to participate in this covenantal relationship as a holy people and a priestly people.

As a holy nation, Israel's role was not to rule over and oppress but to serve in a mediatorial role as a kingdom of priests.

As a holy nation, Israel's role was not to rule over and oppress but to serve in a mediatorial role as a kingdom of priests. The sacred task of serving people as priests is what Israel is corporately called *to do*. Israel's priestly role would serve as a light to the nations as an invitation for others to enter into a relationship with God (Isa. 51:4). This role was for every person in the covenant community! Every person was invited to be holy and to serve as a priest. The idea of a democratized vision for all of humanity harkens back to Genesis 1 where humans are created as image bearers of God. Caring for each other and for God's creation is the sacred task not only of Israelites but of all humanity. As a community of image bearers, as a holy nation, as a kingdom of priests, as a treasured possession and firstborn, biblical Israel was to mediate God's divine presence and purpose in this world. As the story of Exodus continues, these roles will be worked out in specific ways through the construction of the tabernacle, specific priestly functions, laws, and covenant stipulations. In this covenant on Mount Sinai in Exodus 19, it is already clear that all of Israel is invited into this role to mediate God's blessing to the world.

Israel responds to this invitation to covenant relationship with a resounding yes! Moses carries this message before the elders of the community: "Now, therefore, if you obey my voice and keep my covenant, you shall be my treasured possession out of all the peoples" (v. 5, NRSV). Again, the "if" means that the proposition is conditional. This also means that Israel responds willingly and freely. "The people all responded together, 'We will do everything the LORD has said.' So Moses brought their answer back to the LORD" (v. 8, NIV). They are asked to *obey* the Lord and *to keep* the covenant ("obey" in Hebrew is *shema'*, which literally means "to listen").[10] Exodus 19:1 through Numbers 10:10 (the Sinai covenant narrative) will detail a year's worth of instructions to guide their life and practice as they learn to worship and walk in obedience.

---

10. See chapter 5 in this volume by Kevin J. Mellish, "Deuteronomy 6:5."

"Oh, How I Love Your Law!" (Ps. 119:97, NRSV)

Here at the mountain, Israel partners with God in this covenant adventure proposal. They have *defined the relationship*. Next will come more instructions such as laws, the tabernacle project, priestly clothing and duties, and more wilderness adventures. "Law" comes from the word *torah*, which may be better defined as "instructions." In our modern context, laws are legislative. In the ancient context, laws are often hypothetical situations that require wisdom to implement. Israel describes laws as gifts of life (Deut. 6:24). Law is not an abstract, philosophical concept. Laws are relational. Obedience to the law derives from relationship. Israel lives out its calling to be a holy nation and a kingdom of priests through a right relationship with God and with one another.

Living out this calling becomes quite an adventure from Sinai forward! The character Bilbo Baggins in *The Hobbit* describes adventures as "disturbing, uncomfortable things . . . make you late for dinner!"[11] Yes, the Israelites will be uncomfortable at times as they learn to live out this calling in the wilderness. But more than that, they will begin an adventure of *becoming*. Why should the Israelites say yes to this uncomfortable adventure? Because God loves them, has delivered them, and has called them to be God's holy people (Exod. 20:2). The liturgy of remembrance becomes their true north when times get difficult or the future becomes uncertain. *Remember.* The call to remember through activity and worship is built into all of the legal material (e.g., the Ten Commandments [20:1-17], the Covenant Code [20:22–23:19], festivals [34:18-26], Priestly Codes [Lev. 1–16; Num. 1:1–10:10], Holiness Codes [Lev. 17–26], and the Deuteronomic Code [Deut. 12–26]) within the Torah. These instructions are the formational trellis that shapes not only their story but also their formation as a holy people.

Recalling God's mighty acts of deliverance and provision within the context of story continually reminds the Israelites of their continued

---

11. Tolkien, *Hobbit*, 4.

dependence and need for wisdom in living out their priestly roles in their present time. Law is a means of grace and life. Law is a gift, something to meditate on (Ps. 1:2), to take delight in (119:16), and to rejoice over (v. 14), and to love (v. 47)!

This posture helps form the Israelites as image bearers in uncomfortable liminal spaces and places. "Liminal" comes from the Latin word *limen*, meaning "threshold." Israel is continually in these in between, transitional moments of becoming. Israel has witnessed God's glory in Egypt and at Sinai and has beheld God's presence in key moments. God's divine presence is with Israel. God's presence sustains and transforms Israel into a people who are called out to be a blessing to the world. Although the Israelites do not always respond faithfully in the biblical narrative (e.g., the golden-calf episode [Exod. 32]), the Lord continues to be with them, to hear them, and to call them to life as they journey with one another in these middle spaces of "becoming" in order to partner with the Lord to bless and transform the world.

Conclusion

Mount Sinai (Exod. 19) represents a pivotal moment in the Old Testament, a moment where Israel, *as a people*, say yes to the Lord and enter into a covenant relationship. God's mighty hand and outstretched arm (Deut. 4:34) delivers Israel through the Reed Sea. The Lord provides for Israel in the wilderness (Exod. 16). Furthermore, the Lord's presence, care, and commitment in the Exodus stories become the lens through which future stories are shaped and shared throughout the entire biblical corpus.

Do you ever wonder what Moses was most concerned about through all of these Exodus adventures? I think the Sinai story gives us a clue: God's *presence.* When Israel is about to leave Mount Sinai, Moses says, "If your Presence does not go with us, do not send us up from here. How will anyone know that you are pleased with me and with your people unless you go with us? What else will distinguish me and your people from all the other people on the face of the earth?" (33:15-16, NIV). God responds in the intimate context of relationship: "I will do the very thing you have asked, because I am pleased with you and I know you by name" (v. 17, NIV).

God's presence is with Israel and the tabernacle, which is physically set up in the center of camp and is a continual reminder of this spiritual reality. The covenant commitment at Mount Sinai—instructions and liturgy—shapes Israel as a new creation, as God's "firstborn." God's presence through the temple takes on a new understanding in the New Testament as Jesus is revealed as our Immanuel, "God with us" (Matt. 1:23, NIV). Pokrifka writes,

> The Holy Spirit is the presence or glory of God that fills the "temple." Yet "temple" is now redefined as the individual and corporate people of God, rather than any physical structure or building. . . .
>
> . . . The fullest meaning of the tabernacle is fulfilled in the new heaven and the new earth. God will dwell among his holy people in his holy dwelling place, the new Jerusalem (Rev 21:12).[12]

Exodus 19:1-6 is a key moment in the adventure stories of Israel and our own. The trajectory of this mountaintop moment at Sinai reverberates today, as we continue in our calling as a holy people, defined by our status as loved ones (John 13:34-35), image bearers who continue the work to love justice, do mercy, and walk humbly with our God (Mic. 6:8).[13]

Reflection

Exodus 19:1-6 presents the Old Testament theme of God's ongoing presence in the covenant community and the world, past, present, and future. As you reflect on these themes, consider the following:

1. Describe a moment in your life when you remember saying yes to God. Would you see this as a significant DTR moment for you? Discuss what living this out means for you.

---

12. H. Junia Pokrifka, *Exodus*, New Beacon Bible Commentary (Kansas City: Beacon Hill Press of Kansas City, 2018), 432.

13. See chapter 12 in this volume by Beth M. Stovell, "Micah 6:8."

2. The Israelites are formed as a community through some intense moments in the wilderness as they learn to trust God and live obedient lives. Has being part of the community of faith been helpful for you on your personal spiritual journey?

3. Have you experienced moments of God's presence in your journey during transitional seasons in your life? What was significant about this time for you?

4
LEVITICUS 19:2
Derek Davis

Speak to all the congregation of the people of Israel and say to them:
You shall be holy, for I the LORD your God am holy.
—Leviticus 19:2, NRSV

Leviticus 19:2 in the Old Testament

Nothing deters a modern Western reader from completing a full
reading of the Bible more than the first seven chapters of Leviticus. As the
story of the Israelites escaping Egypt comes to a screeching halt with their
arrival at Mount Sinai in Exodus 19, we are plunged into the minutiae of
the wilderness tabernacle construction (chs. 25–40). As the tabernacle
is completed and Exodus concludes, readers are rewarded with the finer
details of taking animals apart for the purpose of participating in the ritual
worship of and reconciliation to the God who had delivered them from
bondage so miraculously. Unfortunately, this is often the end of our exploration of Leviticus.

While the first seven chapters are often a deterrent to modern sen-
sibilities and interest, couched in Leviticus is a core theme that resonates
throughout Scripture. God is attempting to create a habitable space in
which humanity can dwell with God and God with humanity in harmony.
This theme appears first in Genesis 1–3 and culminates in Revelation 21,

but it concentrates in Leviticus: "As the innermost aim of the covenant, dwelling with God in the house of God, for fullness of life in abundant joy and fellowship, is the great promise held out before God's people, and the ardent desire expressed in Israel's liturgy: I will dwell in the house of YHWH for ever (Ps. 23:6)."[1]

Undergirding this biblical theme of dwelling in God's household is the divine command expressed in perhaps the most memorable verse in Leviticus: "Speak to the entire assembly of Israel and say to them: 'Be holy because I, the LORD your God, am holy'" (Lev. 19:2, NIV). The journey of understanding the call for Israel to be holy because God is holy begins with examining the importance of the tabernacle as the house of God into which God's people are invited. The categories of clean/unclean and holy/common in Leviticus also play an important role concerning status and place within the covenant community. It was the duty of the priests to "distinguish between the holy and the common, [and] between the unclean and the clean" (10:10, NIV). And these distinctions help clarify the function and purpose of sacrifice in maintaining peace in the community. All of this provides the context for the call to holiness in Leviticus 19:2 and reveals the importance of hospitality in the form of justice, mercy, and peace as a response to that call. All of these pieces, when assembled, construct a fruitful vision of the call to holiness for God's covenant community.

The Tabernacle

Israel's wilderness tabernacle appears for the first time in Exodus 25–40, and it is assumed as the backdrop for the divine commands and religious ceremonies throughout Leviticus. While it may seem like nothing more than an elaborate tent, it is also a symbol. Its design is nothing short of a microcosm of all creation, meant to signify that just as God created the earth with all of its habitable spaces in Genesis 1, likewise God has

---

1. L. Michael Morales, *Who Shall Ascend the Mountain of the Lord? A Biblical Theology of the Book of Leviticus*, New Studies in Biblical Theology 37 (Downers Grove, IL: InterVarsity Press, 2015), 18.

created this new space in which the people of Israel are invited to dwell together in *shalom*, fully realized peace.[2]

Creation in Genesis 1 began with habitats (day and night, sky and sea, land and vegetation), continued with created things that inhabited those spaces (sun and moon, birds and fish, land mammals and humans), and ended in Sabbath rest. This same rhythm of creation is the rhythm of the worship at the tabernacle, leading the covenant people to rest.[3] The tabernacle as a microcosm of all creation calls God's people back to the creation narrative and to the tranquility found at the beginning of Genesis 3 in the garden of Eden. It is a reminder of God's goal in dwelling among humanity in peace—namely, the restoration of creation and the reconciliation of humanity to God.

Holy and Common, Clean and Unclean

With the tabernacle's symbolic meaning in mind, we may turn our attention to the idea of holiness in Leviticus. If holiness is desired by God to participate ethically in the household God has constructed, what exactly does it entail? One definition identifies holiness as "'that which is unapproachable except through divinely imposed restrictions,' or 'that which is withdrawn from common use.'"[4] With this definition as a framework, the call to be holy, at least in part, implies distinction. God's covenant people must be distinct in their devotion and practices in order to access the holy God. However, this distinction is not exclusionary. Rather, Leviticus is in part a book of processes by which those who might be excluded for various reasons may regain and maintain access. It is also a call to interact ethically with those outside the community, especially through the practice of hospitality as a part of holiness.

---

2. Fretheim, *Exodus*, 269-72.

3. Morales, *Who Shall Ascend?*, 43.

4. Jacob Milgrom, *Leviticus: A Book of Ritual and Ethics*, A Continental Commentary (Minneapolis: Fortress Press, 2004), 107.

Even so, Leviticus enumerates the necessary boundaries for the community to preserve shalom. The boundaries involve separating things into the categories of the holy and the common. Common things are further delineated as either clean or unclean. These statuses can be assigned to a number of things: people, food, pottery, and garments. In Leviticus's rituals involving the tabernacle, something or someone who is common and clean may safely approach that which is holy without danger. However, what is clean can also become unclean. Unclean things have the potential to defile holy objects; or they might invite destruction if they encounter God's holiness. Finally, clean things can be "consecrated" or "sanctified" (both translations of the Hebrew verb meaning "to make holy") and become holy. These are usually objects that became dedicated for use in worship or persons who were consecrated to become priests (or even the high priest) in the tabernacle.[5] For Israel's life as defined in Leviticus, understanding which persons, animals, and objects are clean or unclean, and when, is essential to preserving shalom in the community and to dwelling in God's holy presence, which yields blessing and protection. Throughout Leviticus, Moses provides instructions about the pattern of worship, fellowship, the treatment of illness, natural cycles of life, and diet—all as a way to communicate the boundaries that will govern this community.

Worship and Sacrifice

According to Leviticus, an essential part of maintaining shalom in the community as God's household and of dwelling in God's holy presence is the right worship of God and right fellowship with neighbors. In Leviticus, these two things are ritualized around the tabernacle and find particular expression in the instructions concerning sacrifices and offerings in Leviticus 1–7. Sacrifice in ancient Israel dealt with much more than the forgiveness of sin. The sacrifices and offerings were also a means

---

5. For a more thorough discussion of these categories and how things move from one category to another, see Gordon J. Wenham, *The Book of Leviticus*, The New International Commentary on the Old Testament (Grand Rapids: Eerdmans, 1979), 18-21.

to preserve peace within the community and even to provide food for the participants. For example, the "peace" offering described in Leviticus 3 (from the same Hebrew root word as "shalom") was a sacrifice that provided a portion for God, a portion for the priests, and a portion for the one who brought the offering, suggesting that this was a way of participating in a ritual meal with God and the priests and thus preserving peace.[6] Likewise, what is often translated as the "guilt" offering (5:14-19) may be better translated as the "reparation" offering. It entails making reparations for a wrong someone has done to his or her neighbor. These and the other offerings include an important function of preserving peace with God and within the community.

An essential part of maintaining shalom in the community
as God's household and of dwelling in God's holy
presence is the right worship of God and
right fellowship with neighbors.

Even one of the stranger elements of these sacrifices for modern readers fits with this theme of cultivating peace with God and among God's people. Each of the sacrifices entails that a portion be given to God. And in each one except the reparation offering, this portion is referred to as an offering made by fire (sometimes translated as a "food" offering), creating a pleasing aroma to the Lord. The imagery is that of a meal where the people give homage to their king and the king offers a place at the table. Christian readers may see connections with the imagery of the Last Supper in these passages. Just as Leviticus portrays the people of Israel

---

6. Ibid., 74-75.

bringing their sacrifices to celebrate their ongoing participation in this new kingdom and the promises of God to deliver them, redeem them, and take them into the land, likewise Christians take the bread and the cup to celebrate God's deliverance from the forces of sin and death through Christ's sacrifice, and the promise of being gathered into the new creation to come. This celebration happens in a common meal around the Lord's Table, where we revel in the mystery of God's salvation for all humankind and hear an invitation to dwell in God's household.

The connection of holiness and community in Leviticus includes the specific nuance of how the sacrifices and offerings function to keep peace between God and the people. The process of reconciliation between God and humanity is often called atonement. Although atonement carries some specific meanings in the New Testament (see Heb. 10:19-22), it is multifaceted in Leviticus. Atonement in Leviticus often involves the blood of a clean animal sprinkled on specific parts of the altar and poured out at its base (Lev. 16). Blood is used as a means of expiation—to remove the effects of a person's or community's sins that might pollute the tabernacle and make it impossible for God's holy presence to dwell in the midst of the people. Blood is also used as part of purification rituals after someone has completed their time outside the camp because he or she was exposed to something unclean. In this context, sacrifice commemorates that person's reentry into the community's life. Finally, sacrifice functions as a ransom, the price one pays to redeem something otherwise lost, which recalls the Passover celebration, where God redeemed (or literally "bought back") Israel from their slavery to the Egyptians. This multifaceted nature of sacrifice undergirds the Levitical vision of holiness because it represents an important way that shalom was maintained in the covenant community to ensure all were welcome in God's household.

Holiness as Hospitality in Leviticus 19

The functions of the tabernacle, the categories of holy/common and clean/unclean, and the sacrificial system provide the background for the extended instructions about holiness in Leviticus 19 (esp. vv. 1-18, 33-

34). The call to be holy at the beginning of this chapter is followed by a rendition of the Ten Commandments (cf. Exod. 20:1-17). If holiness is the character of God, who has invited us to live and participate in God's ordered household, it should not be surprising that what follows the opening call to holiness is a list of behaviors that are indicative of God's peaceful community. God's mission is to spread this peace to the whole community of Israel and beyond. In Leviticus 19, we see the command to holiness embodied in hospitality, justice, and mercy in the life of God's people.

Leviticus 19 has a three-part structure: a heading (vv. 1-2), commands (vv. 3-36), and a closing (v. 37). Throughout the commands there are echoes of the key themes previously explored in this chapter. Especially in the commands given in verses 1-18 and 33-34, we find emphases on hospitality toward the family and community, hospitality toward God, and hospitality toward the foreigner and the poor.

Hospitality toward the Family and Community

A holy, hospitable community is characterized by respect for the mother and father and observance of the Sabbath (Lev. 19:3). The household of God is at peace when the many households within it maintain loving order and give space for rest. This is where a community exemplified by holiness begins. The communal expectations continue in verses 11-18, which are summed up well in verse 16b: "Do not do anything that endangers your neighbor's life. I am the LORD" (NIV). The surrounding commands emphasize the need for honesty and justice to be core values of community members by prohibiting lying, stealing, withholding wages, cursing one another, hating one another, or seeking revenge. Leviticus urges community members to judge their neighbors righteously and to forgo the perversion of justice. Without justice, there can be no peace. Without peace, there can be no holiness. Further, the commands urge community members to rebuke one another when transgressions against the community occur in order to mitigate the ritual defilement of the whole community (v. 17).

Verse 18 brings this section to a simple but profound end: "Do not seek revenge or bear a grudge against anyone among your people, but love your neighbor as yourself. I am the LORD" (NIV). The holy community is to share in the divine characteristics. God's people are to be like God. As God loves them, likewise they should love one another in equal measure. God's vision of holiness is encompassed by love; this holy love is what sustains and maintains order within the community and results in peace.

Hospitality toward God

The first commandment that involves how the people relate to God is the prohibition against turning to idols or making "metal gods" (Lev. 19:4, NIV). This is almost certainly meant to evoke the golden-calf incident (Exod. 32) as a reminder that the people often desire a "safer" and less demanding God to appease and placate. The God of Israel does not seek placation. As we explored above about sacrifice, the offerings of Israel were to make reparation, to ransom, and to purify what was previously unclean. Idols represented the temptation for Israel to abdicate its responsibilities and its call to holiness and settle for a mere facade of peace.

A second command that pertains to the divine-human relationship appears in Leviticus 19:5-8. These verses define the acceptable way to partake in the fellowship offering described in Leviticus 3 (referenced as the "peace" offering above). This is the only offering described in Leviticus in which the worshipper (and not just the priest) was allowed to partake of a portion. The instructions found here are to ensure that this meat, which has been made holy through the sacrificial rite, is not desecrated. The punishment for this violation is most severe: the person responsible is to be cut off from the community and that person's sacrifice rendered unacceptable. The desecration of this ritual meal with the family creates a relational divide between God and the worshipper. The call to holiness requires worshippers to take their role seriously in ritual worship. There is no haphazard participation.

Hospitality toward the Foreigner and the Poor

The theme of holiness as hospitality to the poor and the foreigners in the community appears first in what has been traditionally called the gleaning rule (Lev. 19:9-10) or, as Jacob Milgrom alliteratively names it, "horticultural holiness."[7] The community is called to forgo harvesting the edges of its fields and instead to allow for those without land (foreigners and the poor) to have access to the food found there. This divine command simply assumes that the community of holiness has poor and foreign residents within it. The text does not explain why. It simply assumes the reality, and it is the responsibility of the Israelites to care for these members of their community by offering access to food. Additionally, the divine command gives no attention to the injustice of having people who are homeless in a community that is to be characterized by God's holiness. Whatever may be involved in these things, holiness demands that community members care for the needs of these vulnerable persons among them.

Being a redeemed covenant people of God with special access means being outwardly focused and called to serve those on the margins of society.

The final passage to examine in this section is verses 33-34, where caring for foreigners means providing for their general well-being. "Foreigners" (or to avoid the nationalistic sense that term can convey, perhaps "those outside the covenant community") are not to be mistreated. Rather, they are to be considered citizens themselves and to be loved "as yourself" (v. 34, NIV). The reason given for this command to Israel is striking:

---

7. Milgrom, *Leviticus*, 224.

"for you were foreigners in Egypt" (v. 34, NIV). The justification of this requirement suggests a larger theme that could be applied to a number of the preceding commandments. To paraphrase it, one might say, "Do for humanity what God has done for you." In many ways, the call to holiness is a call to interact with and participate in creation as God does.

Being a redeemed covenant people of God with special access means being outwardly focused and called to serve those on the margins of society, just as God rescued Israel from Egypt and has rescued all humanity from bondage to sin and death. As a biblical example from elsewhere, the character of Joseph in Genesis 39–50 exemplifies this kind of holiness. He was the chosen son but did not withhold the blessing from his brothers. Rather, he extended it to those who might be left outside. Here is holiness that loves those on the periphery and gives them a place within the community.

Conclusion

Leviticus 19 calls God's people to holiness. As we have noted, holiness in Leviticus is a complex matter that involves a distinct community dwelling in the household of God and exhibiting the holiness toward others that God exhibited in rescuing it from bondage and freeing it for a life of service to God. Especially in Leviticus 19, the call to holiness emphasizes the importance of hospitality in the form of justice, mercy, and peace as God calls the community to right relationship with itself, God, and those on the periphery. Here is the paradigm of holiness for God's covenant community and the vision of holiness that will culminate in the new creation to come.

Reflection

Leviticus 19 expresses the larger Old Testament themes of the character and life of those of the covenant community (with God and each other), especially through the call to holiness and the promise of God's ongoing presence in the community. To explore how this passage calls God's people today, consider some of these practices and questions:

1. Make a list of personal and communal behaviors and practices that you see congruent with the call to holiness provided in Leviticus 19? Where in these matters is the Spirit calling you to repentance and correction so that you may be a better resident of God's household?

2. An example of holiness in Leviticus 19:9-10 is not gleaning the entirety of an owned field but allowing foreigners and poor persons to come and take food from the crops and field. Describe some practices today that might be comparable to this ancient practice? Why would people resist those practices? How can Christians overcome that resistance?

3. Read Leviticus 19:1-18, 33-34, and Revelation 21. How do you envision the ethics and practices of Leviticus 19 being fulfilled in God's new creation?

5
DEUTERONOMY 6:5
Kevin J. Mellish

You shall love the LORD your God with all your heart,
and with all your soul, and with all your might.
—Deuteronomy 6:5, NRSV

Any volume that attempts to capture the essential message of the Old Testament in representative verses would be incomplete without the inclusion of Deuteronomy 6:4-5. This text, known commonly as the "Shema" in Hebrew tradition, is indispensable for apprehending the heart of Old Testament belief and practice. Theologically, the Shema established the basis for Israel's core understanding of God's nature and spelled out, in concise form, the proper way Israel should relate to God in light of that conviction. Undergirding the Shema is the summons for Israel to have an undivided loyalty to God, and closer inspection of these two verses aids our understanding for the motivation and mandate to serve God wholeheartedly.

Deuteronomy 6:5 in the Old Testament

Deuteronomy is listed as the fifth and final book in the larger collection known as the Torah or Pentateuch. It serves as a capstone to the Torah-Pentateuch because it presupposes Israel's four hundred years of

bondage (Exod. 1–12), the exodus from Egypt (chs. 13–19), the stay
at Mount Sinai (chs. 20–40; Num. 1–9), and the period of wilderness
wandering (Num. 10–36). Deuteronomy provides Moses's final words of
instruction and exhortation before the Israelites enter the promised land
under Joshua (Josh. 1–12). Deuteronomy derives its name from the Greek
deuteros + *nomos*, meaning "second law." This is a fitting title because Deuteronomy represents a restatement and revision of the earlier laws located
in Exodus 20–23. Since God did not allow Moses and the wilderness
generation to cross into Canaan, much of the material in the book is hom-
iletical in style and possesses a forward-looking dimension. Consequently,
the speeches and admonitions contained therein were intended to serve as
guidelines for the Israelites after they had settled down in the land. Based
on the hortatory attributes of Deuteronomy, various scholars have even
classified it as "preached" law.

The book of Deuteronomy contains four main speeches by Moses
(1:1–4:43; 4:44–26:19; 27:1–28:68; 29:1–30:20). Our text under discussion is situated in the second and longest speech, located in 4:44–26:19,
and, more specifically, in the smaller subsection that runs from 5:1 to
11:32. The content and perspective of the second speech distinguish it
from the opening address in 1:1–4:43.

The material in 1:1–4:43 is largely reflective in nature as it recounts
Israel's stay at Mount Horeb (= Sinai) and the journey from Horeb to
the plains of Moab, just outside of Canaan. It also recalls Israel's conflicts
with kings Sihon and Og, as well as the conquest and settlement of the
Transjordan territories (chs. 1–3). The last segment, found in 4:1-40, is
instructional and serves as the conclusion to Moses's first address. It also
shifts the trajectory from the past to the future, from one of wandering to
settlement: "See, just as the LORD my God has charged me, I now teach
you statutes and ordinances for you to observe in the land that you are
about to enter and occupy" (4:5, NRSV). As the closing words of Moses's
first speech, this section offers a powerful exposition on the unique and
all-surpassing character of YHWH (4:7-14) and provides warnings of judgment if the people do not honor YHWH exclusively (4:15-40). Overall,

Moses's opening address highlights the holiness and faithfulness of YHWH while exhorting the Israelites to remain devoted to their God in the land. These themes not only capture the main concerns in chapters 1–4 but are also preparatory for what follows because they lay the foundation for the important teachings set forth in the second address.

Moses's second address in 4:44–26:19 contains two identifiable and interrelated parts. The first section (5:1–11:32) provides the theological basis and impetus for the law code, which follows in the second section (12:1–26:19). While the information in 5:1–11:32 stresses the importance of Israel's obedience to YHWH, the legal material in 12:1–26:19 fleshes out the practical ways Israel honored God in everyday life. When considering the literary relationship between these two sections, it is important to note that the first section begins with the enumeration of the so-called Decalogue (= "ten words") in 5:1-22 (better known as the Ten Commandments). This arrangement is not coincidental, since the core principles set forth in these ten statements (i.e., loving God and loving neighbor) not only established the ideal ethical and moral basis to govern Israel's society but also set the theological tone and agenda for the remainder of the unit (5:23–26:19). The centrality of the Decalogue for religious life is also illustrated by the repeated references to these "statutes" and "ordinances" throughout the remainder of chapter 5: God wrote them down on stone tablets (v. 22), God instructed the people to keep the commandments (v. 29), God delivered the commandments to Moses in order to teach the people (v. 31), and Moses adjured the people to abide by God's commands so that it would go well with them in the land (vv. 32-33). The stress on following God's instruction leads naturally into the section that immediately follows (6:1-3) and is critical for understanding the call to demonstrate exclusive loyalty to YHWH, which is pervasive throughout the rest of chapter 6.

The opening three verses of Deuteronomy 6 just prior to our focus passage directly allude to the Decalogue previously mentioned: "Now this is the commandment—the statutes and ordinances—that the LORD your God charged me to teach you to observe in the land" (v. 1, NRSV). These decrees were intended to serve Israel's best interest, since obedience to YHWH spelled long life in the land for the community (v. 2). Verse 3 concludes this small unit with the charge to follow the statutes and ordinances of verse 1: "Hear therefore, O Israel, and observe them diligently" (v. 3, NRSV). The language in verse 3 ("hear!") not only resembles and reinforces the concerns for obedience to come in verses 4-5 but also stresses the practical benefits of following the message being conveyed. According to verse 3, God will bless the Israelites in the land for observing the ordinances diligently, multiplying them in a land abounding with fertility (i.e., milk and honey) as a result of Israel's faithfulness. The expanded list of blessings mentioned here, as compared to verses 1-2, only stresses the necessity and benefit of obedience to God's teachings. In the verses that immediately follow (vv. 4-5), Israel is called once again to "hear!" as the Shema turns its focus to YHWH and what it means to worship YHWH unconditionally.

The Shema: A Call for Total Commitment

Although just two verses in length, careful exposition of Deuteronomy 6:4-5 reveals a text full of meaning and one that proved theologically formative for the people of God. Verse 4, like the previous verse, begins with the summons to "hear!" In Hebrew, the form of the verb reads as *shema*ʻ, thus giving rise to its namesake. Moreover, the verb is an imperative and meant to grab the attention of the community at large. A common literary and rhetorical construction found in other parts of Deuteronomy (5:1; 9:1; 20:3; 27:9), this verb form conjures up the image of a herald who rallies the people together ("O Israel") for a convocation as a precondition for the delivery of important instruction. The appeal to "hear!" in this context also adds a sense of urgency to the message as it seeks to arouse attentiveness to the proclamation (i.e., "Listen up!" "Pay attention!") and evoke an obedient response to it. Thus the emphasis of this declaration is not just on hearing but on exercising the type of hearing that will elicit active obedience.

The urgency of the command to "hear" in 6:4 is amplified when the reader also takes into consideration the larger literary structure of chapters 5 and 6. The introduction to the Decalogue in 5:1 also begins with the injunction for Israel to "hear" the Ten Commandments God delivered to Moses in verses 7-21. The same verb is then repeated five times in the section that runs from verse 22 to verse 27 and three more times in the unit (5:28–6:3) that immediately precedes our text. Notably, the reference to "hear" in 6:4 represents the tenth time the verb appears between 5:1 and 6:4. This structure is intentional: there are ten utterances (i.e., the Decalogue) following the verb to "hear" in 5:1, with the tenth occurrence of the verb to "hear" culminating in the Shema. It follows, then, that the Shema is presented as a parallel to the Decalogue from the previous chapter. This literary presentation gives added stress to the act of "hearing" in both scenarios; pay attention to the guidelines laid out in 5:7-21, and give heed to the teaching being set down in 6:4-5!

The second half of 6:4 then clarifies more specifically the theological reality that Israel was commanded to heed. The syntax of the verse is admittedly tricky, since it is a verbless construction that literally reads, "YHWH our God, YHWH one." Due to the grammatical vagaries involved, the precise meaning of the phrase has proven elusive to interpreters throughout the centuries and given rise to various interpretations as a result. Most of the confusion and/or debate has centered on the use and meaning of the word "one" (Hebr., *'eḥad*) and the proper way to understand its original intent.

Throughout the interpretive history of this text, scholars have identified two primary ways the second half of the verse has been rendered. The first option takes the word "one" to refer to the unitary nature of Israel's deity. Understood from this perspective, the clause is translated accordingly: "YHWH our God, YHWH is one." This translation accentuates YHWH's singleness of being or internal oneness. Some interpreters have suggested the phrase "YHWH is one" meant that YHWH could not appear or be known in different forms, bear distinct titles (i.e., "YHWH of Samaria" or "YHWH of Teman"), or be worshipped in multiple ways at various sanctuaries. Due to YHWH's unitary nature, the Israelites encountered the same God, or Being, wherever they assembled to venerate YHWH. Others have contended that the singleness of YHWH rejected the notion that there could be a consort or retinue of lesser gods who served as adjuncts to YHWH. This was a common feature in Canaanite religion, which had a reigning supreme deity with other deities serving as helpers or servants.[1] The message of the Shema clearly rejected this idea, since such practices accepted the existence of other deities and recognized their roles in relationship to YHWH.

Finally, some have understood the oneness of YHWH to denote the singleness of YHWH's character. Based on this view, YHWH was one in purpose and integrity. That is to say, YHWH was not duplicitous in purpose or intention.[2] Unlike the mythical deities of Canaanite religion, who could be capricious and fickle in their dealings with humanity, the singleness of YHWH's will and purpose meant that Israel could depend on YHWH to keep oaths and promises. Thus the integrity and faithfulness of YHWH's character were demonstrated in the consistent way YHWH fulfilled covenant obligations. This aspect of YHWH's character was proven time and again in Israel's story as YHWH acted benevolently on behalf of the people, whether in the redemption from sin or the exodus from Egypt.[3]

The second, and more predominant, way interpreters have understood the phrase "YHWH is one" centers on YHWH's *authority*. Based on this reading, the phrase can be translated, "YHWH (is) our God, YHWH alone." This translation stresses the fact that Israel recognized and worshipped only one deity, YHWH. In a world where polytheism abounded, the Shema prohibited the Israelites from worshipping the gods of the na-

---

1. Ronald E. Clements, "The Book of Deuteronomy," in *The New Interpreter's Bible Commentary* (Nashville: Abingdon, 2015), 1:906.

2. Richard D. Nelson, *Deuteronomy: A Commentary*, The Old Testament Library (Philadelphia: Westminster John Knox Press, 2004), 89.

3. J. Gerald Janzen, "On the Most Important Word in the Shema," *Vetus Testamentum* 37, no. 3 (1987): 280-300.

tions around them (see also Exod. 20:3; Deut. 5:7: "no other gods before/ in front of me"). YHWH was "unique" compared to the gods of Israel's neighbors and therefore worthy of Israel's complete loyalty and devotion. Israel honored YHWH exclusively because YHWH was superior in rank, power, and holiness to all other deities.

In light of these interpretive options, the imperative to "love" YHWH in verse 5 makes perfect sense. Here the specifications of Israel's devotion to YHWH are spelled out more fully. The terms of Israel's obedience are made clear: "You will love YHWH your God with all your heart, and with all your soul, and with all your might." The call to love is also an imperative, since the force of the command to "hear" in the previous verse carries over to the beginning of verse 5.

Although it may seem counterintuitive for love to appear in a command form, it is not unusual in the Old Testament (see 11:1, 13, 22). "Love" in Hebrew (*'ahab*) should not be immediately identified with emotion, feeling, or sentiment. Although it can refer to the love between a man and a woman (Gen. 24:67), the concept of love is more commonly associated with the virtues of loyalty, commitment, and obedience. In the ancient world, the language of "love" was used in the realm of political relationships and conveyed the notion of faithfulness or devotion (1 Kings 5:1). Thus to "love" YHWH meant Israel was expected to be fully committed to YHWH as a covenant partner.

The injunction further calls upon Israel to love YHWH with all of the "heart," "soul," and "might." In order to appreciate the meaning of this terminology, it is necessary to consider the basic definition of these terms. In Hebrew thought, the "heart" (Hebr., *leb*) was much more than a physical organ located in the chest cavity. This was the organ in which the vital aspects of a person's inner being were located. It represented the inner core or personality, the invisible aspects of the total person.[4] As such the heart was the seat of the feelings, the will, desire, and the intellect. At the

---

4. Ian Cairns, *Deuteronomy: Word and Presence*, International Theological Commentary (Grand Rapids: Eerdmans, 1992), 84.

emotional level, the heart was the place where a person felt distress (Ps. 25:17), anguish (25:17), fear (Deut. 20:8; Josh. 7:5; Isa. 7:2, 4), confidence (Ps. 27:14), sadness (1 Sam. 1:8), and joy (Isa. 30:29). The heart is where one experienced a sense of longing (Ps. 21:2) and desire (Prov. 6:25). In addition, the heart held the capacity for reason, intellect (Deut. 29:4), wisdom (Ps. 90:12), consciousness (Jer. 17:1), reflection (Ps. 77:6), and understanding (Job 34:10).[5] It was also where inclinations (Gen. 6:5), the conscience (1 Sam. 24:5), and one's intentions (2 Sam. 7:3) resided. A person had the ability and freedom to demonstrate inflexibility toward God (Exod. 7:3, "hardness of heart") or choose repentance (2 Chron. 34:27, "a soft heart"). Therefore, when some Old Testament passages refer to the circumcision of the heart, they imply one who returns or surrenders to YHWH (Deut. 10:16) in genuine devotion (Jer. 3:10).

In addition to the heart, the text instructs the Israelites to love YHWH with all of the soul. The term for "soul" in Hebrew (*nepesh*) does not mean the immortal part of the personality that survives death, as is commonly thought. Rather, the term is connected to the throat-neck area and corresponds to the physical needs of a person. As such, the *nepesh* requires food or water (Eccles. 6:7) and rest (2 Sam. 16:14). The *nepesh* represented the life (i.e., as the throat took in air) of a person (Gen. 35:18), which could be threatened by drowning (Jon. 2:5). Like the heart, the *nepesh* related to one's appetites, desires, and will. Thus one who was stubborn or obstinate and resisted God was called "stiff necked" (Exod. 32:9; Jer. 17:23). Moreover, the *nepesh* was a repository for emotions and spiritual experiences. In the *nepesh*, one experienced suffering (Job 19:2), sympathy (30:25), fear (Ps. 6:3), hate (2 Sam. 5:8), and love (Song of Sol. 1:7; 3:1-4). It was in the *nepesh* that a person also expressed a desire or longing for God (Isa. 26:9; Ps. 42:1) and exulted in the Lord (Ps. 35:9).

---

5. In many respects, the "heart" in Hebrew anthropology corresponds to the mind in Western thought. It was not by accident that Jesus, who was living in a Greco-Roman world, recited the Shema as loving God with all the heart, soul, *mind*, and strength (Mark 12:29-31).

As a final exhortation, the Israelites were instructed to love God with all their "might" (Hebr., *me'od*). The Hebrew term has often been translated as "strength," as is attested in many modern versions (NIV, NLT, NKJV, NASB). However, when considering the origins of the word, *me'od* conveys the notion of "force" or "abundance." Taken literally, it means to love God "with muchness." Understood from this perspective, the language refers to the intensity by which the people are to love and obey God. The term "is a single-minded, love-inspired zeal and determination to realize the whole will of God."[6] Taken together, then, these three terms imply that loving YHWH requires a total commitment of the whole person: mind, will, desire, intensity, and emotion.

Wholehearted Devotion in Deuteronomy

The message of wholehearted devotion to YHWH in Deuteronomy 6:4-5 is spelled out in greater detail throughout the book. What did it mean for Israel to honor God according to the commands set forth in the Shema? Whether in Moses's sermons, the central law code, or reflective summaries, Deuteronomy laid out practical ways Israel could fulfill the mandates of our focus text. Chapter 7, for example, reminded the people that God loved them and chose (v. 7) them out of all the peoples of the earth. As a result, they were to remain distinct from the people of the land, reject their religious customs and practices, and refuse to intermingle with them or else their hearts would turn after their gods (vv. 2-6). In other parts of the book, the people were required to tear down the pagan altars and shrines throughout the land and worship YHWH at the designated sanctuary (12:2-7). Various types of pagan practices, whether Canaanite mourning rites (14:1-2), child sacrifice, divination, or magic (18:9-14), were expressly prohibited. Likewise, worshipping other gods was completely forbidden. Deuteronomy contains some of the harshest legislation for those who would entice the Israelites to go after foreign dei-

---

6. Cairns, *Deuteronomy*, 85.

ties, whether it was a prophetic figure (13:1-5); someone in the community, including family members (vv. 6-11); or "scoundrels" in the towns that God gave the Israelites to inhabit (vv. 12-18, NRSV). Anyone who violated these precepts was subject to severe discipline in order to purge the evil from Israel's midst.

The emphasis on exclusive loyalty is understandable, since YHWH represented Israel's true Lord, who required unconditional obedience. This expectation derived from the political world of the ancient Near East, where covenant relationships were formed. In biblical times, covenant agreements existed in two primary forms: the parity treaty and the suzerain (or vassal) treaty. According to the terms of a parity treaty, both parties entered the relationship on equal terms. Since one party could not lord over the other, both participants related to one another as equals. In a suzerain treaty, however, the suzerain functioned as the superior party while the vassal took on the role of the servant (or client). In this type of political arrangement, the servant demonstrated loyalty to the suzerain, because the suzerain performed benevolent actions on behalf of the less powerful client. Israel's relationship to God shares many parallels with the suzerain-client covenant agreement. Moreover, the book of Deuteronomy is organized according to the parameters of the suzerain treaty known from the ancient world. The outline below demonstrates the typical layout of such a treaty and how the parts of Deuteronomy resemble that layout:

1. *Preamble.* The great king identified himself and provided his name and titles (Deut. 1:1-5; see also Exod. 20:2*a*, "I am YHWH, your God").

2. *The Historical Prologue.* The king recited the historical basis for the treaty, identifying gracious activity done on behalf of the client (Deut. 1:6–11:32; see also Exod. 20:2*b*, "who brought you out of the land of Egypt, out of the house of slavery" [NRSV]).

3. *Conditions or Stipulations of the Treaty.* The terms of the relationship or agreement were spelled out in detail for the servant (Deut. 12–26).

4. *Preservation and Public Proclamation of the Treaty.* The treaty was written down, and the covenant was renewed and read aloud periodically (Deut. 27:1-10; 31:10-13).

5. *Witnesses of the Treaty Listed.* Deities were called upon to witness the agreement. In the case of Israel's covenant with God, heaven and earth were called upon as witnesses to testify against Israel for breaches of the contract (Deut. 30:19; 32:1; see also Mic. 1:2).

6. *List of Blessings and Curses.* The covenant outlined blessings for obedience to the treaty agreement and listed curses (punishments) for breach of the terms (Deut. 27:1–28:68).

Exclusive loyalty to YHWH entailed not only the rejection of the gods and religious customs of the nations but a call to exhibit love and devotion to YHWH.

By structuring Deuteronomy along these lines, the writers and editors of the book underscored YHWH's role as Israel's divine Lord (suzerain) and Israel's status as YHWH's servant. Just as the suzerain treaty required total obedience by the servant, so Israel was bound to honor YHWH with wholehearted devotion.

Exclusive loyalty to YHWH entailed not only the rejection of the gods and religious customs of the nations but a call to exhibit love and devotion to YHWH in other meaningful ways according to Deuteronomy. For example, the book challenged the people to honor YHWH with the admonition to "remember" (Hebr., *zakhar*). Not only were the people required to "hear" (i.e., listen and obey) God's instruction, but they were also exhorted to "remember" what YHWH had done for them in the past and what YHWH would do for them in the future. Israel was called to reflect on how God delivered them from Egyptian bondage (6:21-23; 11:3-4) and faithfully led them through the wilderness (11:5-7). Recollecting God's gracious activity on behalf of Israel was imperative because God's benevolent actions served as the foundation for the covenant and the basis for Israel's grateful response in obedience to YHWH. Remembering was not just about the past, however. Deuteronomy instructed Israel to be sure to remember God after settling in the promised land. After eating their fill, living in fine houses, and watching their flocks and herds multiply, the Israelites must not forget that God provided all of their material blessings (8:12-18). Forgetting that God was responsible for Israel's good fortune would cause the people to "follow other gods to serve and worship them" (v. 19, NRSV).

In Deuteronomy, the act of remembering God's goodness was also tied to religious activities by which the people demonstrated their gratitude to God. Israel demonstrated covenant loyalty to YHWH through the presentation of their offerings and tithes and in the celebration of yearly festivals. Each year, the people set apart a portion (tithe) of the yield from the harvest to give to God as an act of worship and to support the sanctuary and ministry personnel (14:22-27). In addition, the people commemorated God's saving, liberating action in the exodus by offering the Passover sacrifice at the sanctuary each year (16:1-8). The festival of weeks, or Pentecost, served as a harvest festival in early summer when the first fruits of the grain were presented in the sanctuary (vv. 9-12). Moreover, in the autumn festival of Sukkoth (booths), the community presented a share of the crops at the end of the agricultural year (vv. 13-15). Significantly, these offerings were to be dedicated to God with a generous and glad spirit; they were to be offered with sincere gratitude. When the people presented their gifts to YHWH, they were instructed to "rejoice before the LORD your God—you and your sons and your daughters, your male and female slaves, the Levites resident in your towns, as well as the strangers, the orphans, and the widows who are among you" (v. 11, NRSV; see also 14:26; 16:14).

King Josiah: A Leader Who Fulfilled the Demands of the Shema

The command to follow YHWH wholeheartedly in the Shema is exemplified best in the leadership of King Josiah (2 Kings 22–23). No king followed the command to love and follow YHWH with the whole being the way Josiah did. Josiah is known for being an incomparable king who led a thoroughgoing revival among the people. Josiah's revival did not happen by accident, however, and the events that prompted Josiah's reform are noteworthy.

Josiah was just a child when he became king over the Southern Kingdom (Judah) in 641 BCE. In his eighteenth year, he sent his officials to the temple in Jerusalem to provide funds to repair the structure. At this time, Hilkiah, the high priest, reported to Josiah's secretary that he had discovered the book of the Torah-Law in the temple. The secretary, Shaphan, then brought this Torah-Law before Josiah and "read it aloud to the king" (22:10, NRSV). The Torah-Law that Shaphan read before Josiah was most likely a form of Deuteronomy, and when Josiah "heard" the words from this book, he tore his clothes and sent his officials to consult the woman prophet Huldah for her spiritual guidance. Huldah affirmed that Josiah had indeed received the word of God. The message Josiah heard prompted him not only to respond in contrition but also to gather all the people, along with the priests and prophets, and to read to them the sacred words from the book. In addition, he led the community in a covenant-renewal ceremony, whereby the people pledged an oath of loyalty to YHWH. As evidence of the sincerity of Josiah's devotion, he then aggressively went about restoring the proper veneration of YHWH throughout the land.

Josiah, inspired by the message he heard, enacted a reform that rectified the religious abuses of the past, even those going back to the days of Solomon. He not only removed the high places that Solomon had set up for foreign deities but also got rid of the idolatrous priests, smashed the images devoted to Canaanite gods and goddesses, defiled Topheth (the place where child sacrifice took place), and pulled down the pagan altars that the evil kings Ahaz and Manasseh had erected. He also demolished the altar and high place that the northern king Jeroboam had set up at Bethel, the very shrine that caused the Northern Kingdom (Israel) to turn away from YHWH.

In addition to these sweeping changes, Josiah made sure that the people celebrated Passover as an integral part of his reform—the same festival prescribed in the book of Deuteronomy (16:1-8). Josiah is the only ruler in 1 and 2 Kings who led the people in the Passover ceremony. He epitomized the message of the Shema in the way that he demonstrated his devotion to YHWH after he "heard" the words of YHWH read to him. The text even verifies this in the way it remembers Josiah's righteous reign: "Before him there was no king like him, who turned to the LORD with all his heart, with all his soul, and with all his might, according to all the law of Moses" (2 Kings 23:25, NRSV). These words reveal that Josiah knew what it meant to love and honor YHWH with wholehearted devotion.

Reflection

Deuteronomy 6:4-5 expresses the larger Old Testament themes of God's saving work for Israel and the character and life of the covenant community (especially through the call to wholehearted devotion). Consider some of these practices and questions concerning the calling upon God's people today:

1. Deuteronomy 6:4 reminds us that God intended the message from the text to be heard by the community of faith. Try reading Deuteronomy 6:4-5 out loud and listening to it being read. Reading the text audibly or hearing it read aloud allows us to hear God's word in a new, meaningful, and challenging way. Remember, active hearing is not just about listening but also about putting the message received from the text into action.

2. What are some concrete examples of loving God in the way the Shema commands—with your whole being, encompassing the mind, will, and emotions?

3. Deuteronomy challenged the people to remember what God had done for them in the past and what God would do for them in the future. Write down the ways God has helped you, answered prayer, or blessed your life in former times so that you can remember God's goodness and provision in the present and future.

6
2 SAMUEL 7:13
Stephen P. Riley

> *[The LORD], himself, will build a house for my name,*
> *and I will establish the throne of his kingdom forever.*
> —2 Samuel 7:13

"For-ev-er!" That is what the young baseball player Squints in the movie *The Sandlot* says as he explains that anything that goes over the fence of Mr. Mertle's yard becomes the property of the "Beast." The kids are terrified that if they hit a baseball into Mr. Mertle's backyard, the big dog will never let them get their ball back. The focus passage of this chapter, 2 Samuel 7:1-17, has at least one connection to that scene. In our text, King David, after capturing Jerusalem and bringing the ark of God into the city, decides to build God a house. But the prophet Nathan is called upon to deliver God's message to David that he will not be the one to build God's house. During the prophet's message, however, we find out that it will be David's offspring who will build a house for God's name. We also learn that God promises to make David a "house" or, more clearly, descendants who will be established on the throne "forever."

In this chapter, we will explore the importance of 2 Samuel 7:1-17 within Israel's canonical story and a few implications for how we can interpret it for our lives today as part of God's continuing story with us.

Our Text: 2 Samuel 7:1-17

Our text is significant for several reasons; however, it is most notable because of the promise God makes to David in it. In the previous chapters of 2 Samuel, David has moved the capital from Hebron to Jerusalem, been anointed as king over all Israel, and moved the ark of God to Jerusalem. This last move solidified Jerusalem as the political and religious center of all Israel during David's reign, unifying the people after years of tribal conflict. Now, as David perceives a sense of peace and unity, he seeks to build a house of cedars for the Lord to sit in and establish Jerusalem as the place where the heavens and earth connect (7:1-2).

At first, it appears that David will get his desire as he seeks the counsel of his prophet Nathan. Nathan says, "Everything that is in your heart, go. Do. For the LORD is with you" (v. 3). It is worth noting that neither David nor Nathan inquires of the Lord about whether this is something God desires. David apparently goes in search of a solution to a problem that may not have existed. They simply assumed that God's ark residing in a tabernacle was insufficient. This concept, though, was common in ancient Western Asia. Kings would often establish their kingdoms by building temples for their gods and giving a physical representation of divine blessing on their rule.

Nathan's response is, perhaps, more troubling. As a prophet, he should have inquired of God on behalf of the king, seeking God's answer to the question. However, he simply responds in the affirmative to David. This may be a way the narrator is giving us a clue about Nathan and the way he engages in prophetic activity. Prophets were supposed to be the spokespersons for the Lord, not those who simply affirmed what people in power wished. On the other hand, it may be that Nathan simply believed that what David requested was legitimate and without problem. Whatever the case, in the next verse the Lord appears to Nathan and speaks to the prophet. In the ensuing verses there are two distinct speeches. The first speech, contained in verses 5-7, deals with God's denial of David's request about the temple. The second speech, verses 8-16, covers God's promise to establish David's "house," with the additional promise that one of David's offspring will build a house for God's name.

In the first speech, the Lord tells Nathan to remind David that the Lord has never asked for a place to reside and is not doing so now. In fact, the prophet is told that the Lord has been "walking around" in a tent and tabernacle since the days of the Exodus (v. 6). The apparent issue at hand is the nature of God's presence. By building a house for the Lord, it seems that David wishes to control God's presence by locating it on his terms. The Lord, on the other hand, has never been controllable in the biblical narrative. Indeed, the Lord has always been on the move in order to care for the people of God and, thus, will not be controlled by a king or anyone else. The building of the temple must be for a purpose different from that of solidifying one's personal power.

Building a house for God's name is
a form of worship and honor.

The second speech, however, gives hope for David and his line. In this speech, the Lord takes center stage by reminding David of the Lord's acts of salvation. The Lord specifically speaks of how David was raised from the lowly status of being a shepherd in the fields to the lofty status of being a leader of God's people. More importantly, the Lord has constantly been with David throughout his journey, protecting him from his enemies and making his name great in all the earth (vv. 9-10). From there the speech transitions to a discussion about how the Lord appointed a place for the Israelites to dwell, highlighting how the Lord has cared for them, brought them to the promised land, and caused them to have rest and safety (vv. 10-11). This rehearsal of God's work among the people is consistent with covenantal language, setting up the promises the Lord will make to David in the next verses. After that, in verse 12, the Lord promises to make a "house" for David. This will not be a literal house, like the one David proposed, but a line of descendants through whom the Lord will establish the kingdom.

At this point in the speech our highlighted verse takes center stage. In verse 13, the Lord states, "He, himself, will build a house for my name, and I will establish the throne of his kingdom forever." This contains several important points for understanding the Old Testament. First, the Lord states that it is one of David's offspring who will build a house. Although David is certainly recognized as one of the great kings of Israel, he is not the one who built the temple. I've suggested that our text makes an important distinction between making a house for God and a house for God's name. While some might say that God and God's name are the same, various commentators have pointed out that building a house for God's name is different from building a house for God to reside in. In essence, building a house for God to reside in is a form of control over God, while building a house for God's name is a form of worship and honor.

Second, the Lord will establish the throne of David's child's kingdom forever. This promise is later repeated in verse 16, where the Lord states that the child will be "established in your house and your kingdom forever before you; your throne will be established forever." This type of promise reflects covenant language between a god and a human in ancient Western Asia. This type of covenant occurs when a divine being makes an unconditional promise. In the Old Testament we have seen this before. God made a similar covenant with Noah in Genesis when God promised never to destroy the earth again with a flood. God also promised Abraham innumerable descendants and land for them in Genesis 15.

In both instances God's promise came without any expectations. Our text reflects a similar situation, as God makes two promises to David without requiring anything in return. This is important, because within this history of Israel, the framework of God's covenant with God's people always requires something in return. In Deuteronomy, Moses tells the people that for them to live in the land God has promised, they must faithfully love God with all their heart, mind, and strength and must obey all God's commandments. In this case, God simply makes a promise to David and asks nothing in return. From the context in which Israel was reading its history, this promise was particularly important. Because the Israelites were reading their history from a place of exile and suffering, remembering that God had promised David that there would be an heir of his on the throne forever might have given the people hope that God had not abandoned them or the monarchy. For the early readers of the text, remembering that God would fulfill this promise to David offered hope and a reason to trust God's continued work in and through them. It was a reminder that God's purposes for this world were not defeated by the armies of the Babylonians; even in the exile there was still a reason for the people to live faithfully before God as they rebuilt their lives and looked toward the future.

2 Samuel 7:13 in the Old Testament

In order to understand this hope and how our text functions as part of the Old Testament, we must locate it within the larger canon. Our text is part of a larger literary narrative, often referred to as the Deuteronomistic History, which is a fancy way of saying the history of Israel through the theology of Deuteronomy. This theological history is comprised of the biblical texts of Deuteronomy, Joshua, Judges, 1 and 2 Samuel, and 1 and 2 Kings. As a narrative about Israel's past, these combined texts appear to be an attempt to explain how Israel ended up in Babylon after the destruction of Jerusalem in 586 BCE. Theologically speaking, the texts are unified by some common themes such as absolute loyalty to the God of Israel, complete avoidance of anything to do with the worship of foreign gods, worship of God only at Jerusalem, and faithfulness to the regulations and teachings of Moses found in Deuteronomy 12–26 specifically.

These themes of Deuteronomistic History are woven into the various books in several ways. Unfortunately, what the history mostly shows is how the Israelites' unfaithfulness ultimately led to their expulsion from the land God had given to them. The hope of the storytellers is that by reading this history, the Israelites would be reminded of their past and choose to live differently. The goal was to help the returning exiles live as a faithful people to God in the rebuilt Israel.

It is helpful to know the broader story of the Deuteronomistic History because of this context. The story begins with Moses's final speech to the people on the east side of the Jordan River. The book of Deuteronomy recounts this speech in which Moses exhorts the people to be completely faithful to the Lord. A primary text from this book is known as the "Shema," which comes from the Hebrew word for "hear," found in Deuteronomy 6:4-5: "Hear, Israel! The LORD, our God, the LORD is one. And you will love the LORD your God with all your heart and with all your life and with all your strength." This text sets the tone for the rest of the history. The Israelites are supposed to love God with everything they have. However, after Moses's death, things begin to fall apart.

In the book of Joshua, the new leader Joshua can help the people inherit the promised land. At the end of the book, Joshua calls the people together and reconfirms the covenant the people have made with God. Following Joshua's death, the book of Judges tells the story of Israel's consistent downward rebellious spiral. The story moves through a cycle of judges who deliver the people only to see them do evil again. By the end of the book, there is no more deliverance; there is only a civil war between the tribes, and everyone is doing what is right in his or her own eyes. Following Judges, the books of Samuel tell of the rise and fall of Israel's final judge-like leaders and its first monarch, Saul. After Saul's rejection as king, David arises in the narrative. His story is a complex one complete with moments of entire faithfulness to God followed by utter failure. David's story ends in the first part of the books of Kings as he hands the kingdom over to his son Solomon. At the apex of the united monarchy, Solomon can build a temple for God's name in Jerusalem and dedicate it with language reminiscent of Moses and Joshua. The story turns after Solomon's death, and the kingdom splits in two. The rest of the narrative in the books of Kings follows the downward spiral of first the Northern Kingdom, Israel, who has no good kings, and then the Southern Kingdom, Judah.

The Northern Kingdom is exemplified by its first king, Jeroboam I, who builds golden calves at two shrines, Dan and Bethel, for his people to use for worship. The Northern Kingdom ends in 722 BCE when the Assyrians, under Shalmaneser V, capture Samaria and terminate the reign of Hoshea. In the south, Judah continues for another 136 years. In that time, two significant kings are highlighted in 2 Kings. First, Hezekiah is a king that responds faithfully to God during a crisis. In 701 BCE, the Assyrians march on Jerusalem. Hezekiah, urged by the prophet Isaiah, turns to God and trusts God to deliver the people. Amazingly, one morning the people wake up to find the Assyrians gone and the siege over. Second, almost sixty years later, it is after the boy king Josiah has grown into adulthood that a second revival occurs. Josiah is credited with rebuilding the temple and finding a copy of the Torah of Moses. After having it read, Josiah begins a revival of Torah obedience that includes celebrating the Passover. He is thus known as one of the greatest kings in Israel's history because he helped turn Judah back to serving God. During his reign, language that mirrors theology from Deuteronomy permeates his story. For example, Josiah is said to have been a king that "put away all the detested idols that were seen in the land of Judah and in Jerusalem. . . . Before him there was no king like him, who returned to the LORD with all his heart, with all his soul, and with all his might according to all the Torah of Moses" (2 Kings 23:24-25).

Unfortunately, Josiah is killed in battle. Israel relapses into old patterns and forgets to follow the Lord. Finally, after a series of bad kings, Nebuchadnezzar and the Babylonians deport much of the population of Jerusalem and destroy the temple and city in 586 BCE. The final chapters of 2 Kings give significant attention to these events, especially the destruction of the temple. At the end of the story, the narrator relates the circumstances of Jehoiachin, one of David's heirs, who is living in exile and eating at the table of the Babylonian king, Evil-merodach. This ending has been interpreted in various ways, but one thing to note is the possibility that a Davidic heir could still return to the throne, which is significant for our passage.

The Context of Our Text in the Books of Samuel

Examining the books of Samuel more closely one notices how important they are within Israel's story. They give a particular picture of the origins of Israel's kingship. In order to understand the story, one has to clearly grasp the importance of one of the first narratives in the book. The first book of Samuel begins with a narrative about Hannah, a barren woman, who prays to God for a child. When her request is granted, she offers a psalm of thanksgiving to God that includes these lines: "The Lord! Making poor, making rich, making low, more so raising up!" (1 Sam. 2:7), and "Let [God] give strength to his king and raise high the horn of his anointed one" (v. 10). These lines highlight a main theme of the books of Samuel: the rise and fall of leading characters and the setup for David to become the anointed leader of Israel.

The Context of Samuel before David's Story

Three significant characters—Eli, Samuel, and Saul—rise and fall from the narrative before David comes to the forefront of the story. Each one comes onto the scene in some fashion as a leader of Israel but is ultimately found incapable of leading the people in the ways of God. Eli is presented as one who cannot see the evil his two sons do as priests. Therefore, his downfall is brought about when the ark of God is taken by the Philistines. Samuel is raised up as the new leader of Israel, and his word leads the people for a long time. He leads the people as a judge and prophet-like figure. Throughout his story, Samuel encourages the people to be faithful to God.

However, the people, wanting to be like all the other nations, desire a king, and Samuel consents to their wishes. As Saul is anointed the first legitimate monarch of Israel, Samuel begins to fade into the background of the narrative. However, with his final speech in 1 Samuel 12, Samuel again encourages the people to be faithful to God with language consistent with the Deuteronomistic theology: "Surely, fear the LORD and serve him with faithfulness and with all your heart because see what he has made great with you! However, if you indeed do evil, also you and your king will be swept away" (vv. 24-25). With Saul, things look promising at first. He is able to rally a significant portion of Israel to work together for military victory at Jabesh-gilead.

However, Saul oversteps his role and offers a sacrifice before a battle, which is something reserved for religious officials, drawing the ire of Samuel in chapter 13. Samuel says,

> You have acted foolishly. You have not kept the LORD your God's commandments, which he commanded you; for now, the LORD has established your kingdom to Israel forever. But now, your kingdom will not stand. The LORD has sought for himself a man like his heart, and he commanded him to be a ruler over his people, for you did not keep that which the LORD commanded you. (Vv. 13-14)

This language of rejection is clearly in line with the Deuteronomistic ideal of a king who follows God's commands in everything. Deuteronomy 17:14-20 is commonly referred to as the "law of the king." These verses outline the notion of an ideal king for Israel. For Israel, a king should be an Israelite who does not gain much wealth, women, or military prowess. Most importantly, the king should have a copy of the Torah (likely similar to our book of Deuteronomy) read for him on a regular basis in order to help him remain completely faithful to the Lord. Hence, when Saul is rejected as king and Samuel says the Lord is looking for a "man like his heart," that language is drawn from the law of the king and sets the reader up for David to appear in the narrative. From the rejection of Saul going forward, David becomes the primary actor in the story.

The Context of David's Story in Samuel

As David's story rises in Samuel, what becomes prominent is his chosen status. An early narrative about David highlights this theme. While Saul is still king, David goes to the battlefield where the giant Goliath is taunting the Israelite army. Although Saul tries to give David his armor and warns him of the danger, David simply goes out to meet the giant with a slingshot and his trust in God. After prevailing in battle, the people begin to sing songs about David, saying, "Saul has killed his thousands, but David has killed ten thousand" (1 Sam. 18:7).

Later, while fleeing from Saul's rage, David continually finds people who will help him as they recognize him as the legitimate anointed ruler. For example, as he is fleeing, he comes upon a man named Nabal. While there, Abigail, Nabal's wife, recognizes David as the chosen one and says, "The LORD will indeed make for my lord [referring to David] a firm house," and later, "when it happens that the LORD does for my lord according to all the good things which the LORD spoke about you, and the LORD commands you to be a leader over Israel" (1 Sam. 25:28-30). It is important to recognize in this speech by Abigail that she uses the same language used in our passage. She says that the Lord will make David a "firm house," which means an established line of descendants. This is the same language that Nathan uses to describe the promise God makes to David in our passage. Similarly, Abigail says that David will be a "leader over Israel." This term "leader" is a special Hebrew word. It is a rare word, *nagid*, which is translated in a few ways by different Bible translators. However, the basic sense of the word is "prince" or "leader." This is the same language that is used in our passage. The idea that the Lord is establishing David and his heirs as a house that will care for Israel is a theme the author highlights throughout the story.

Later, in 2 Samuel 5, all the Israelites gather at Hebron to make a covenant with David and anoint him as king. While there, they say, "During the time of Saul's reigning over us, it was you going out and bringing in Israel. The LORD said to you, 'You will shepherd my people, Israel, and you will be a leader [*nagid*] for Israel'" (v. 2). The portrait of David as a shepherd-leader is important because it aligns with Deuteronomy's law of the king as well as other texts about the ideal image of what God desires for humanity's way of being in the world. If one remembers, the first command God gives the first humans is to "be fruitful and multiply, fill the earth, and *have dominion* over it" (Gen. 1:28; emphasis added). The word that is used for "have dominion" is a word with royal associations. It means to care for and protect something as a monarch would. It is interesting, then, that the ideal king is one who protects as a shepherd who is supposed to understand God's Torah and not collect the various symbols of power and strength many monarchs would have collected in ancient Western Asia.

The unfortunate reality of David's line and Israel is that within the following chapters of 2 Samuel, David is engaged in significant violence, sexual abuse, murder, and a cover-up. Following the confrontation by the prophet Nathan in chapter 12, David learns that the sword will never leave his house, which turns out to be true. For the rest of his life, David is besieged by one horrific family event or national crisis after another. Even in David's death, his children fight for the throne as David attempts to pass the kingdom on. The end of his life sets the tone for the rest of the history of the monarchy, which we have already seen ends with the destruction of two capitals and the temple. This all opens the question for us, What might we learn from this portion of the Old Testament that can help us live faithfully before God today?

Implications of Our Text

There are two points I want to make about our text as it relates to understanding the Old Testament. First is to highlight how this text demonstrates God's grace in the Old Testament. Second is to show how this text sets up a judgment marker for the rest of the kings in Israel. Then there are two themes I want to highlight that I believe will help us live faithfully before God today.

Understanding the Old Testament through 2 Samuel 7:1-17

This passage is important for understanding Israel's sense of its past. Reading and interpreting history from such a distance in time and place is always difficult. However, it seems clear that with this text Israel was, for one thing, trying to highlight its belief that God certainly would work in and through fragile human beings and through flawed institutions such as a monarchy. I do not believe this text endorses everything David or his line did. Nor do I believe God endorses the monarchy or any other political structure as an institution for all times and places. It is helpful, however, to recognize that Israel believed that God could work through things that may not be God's best plan. As such, as we read the history of Israel through Deuteronomy's eyes, we recognize that there is much grace in Israel's story. Israel tells a story of God trying to work with and through Israel, often in terrible and difficult situations, to accomplish the covenant God made with Abraham and Sarah back in Genesis.

Israel believed that God could work through things that may not be God's best plan.

Second, it is worth noting that this passage sets up a point of reference for the rest of the history of the monarchy in Israel. Throughout the rest of the narrative in the books of Kings, all kings in Jerusalem (also known as Judah during the two kingdoms and then Israel again after the Northern Kingdom is destroyed) are judged according to how well they walk the ways of David. Though David's story takes some particularly unfortunate turns after this moment, the history remembers David as the one in covenant relationship with the Lord. Therefore, kings are judged theologically—not politically—based on how well they live in covenant with the Lord.

Two Themes to Consider for Faithful Living Today

The first theme for faithful living to explore from the text is how God calls upon David to be a leader for Israel. I want to state up front that I fear writing about leadership because it has often been divorced from discipleship. However, what I think David was being called to was not power and privilege or any type of modern understanding of a leader. As mentioned before, the term used in the text is a somewhat unique term, suggesting a prince or leader for Israel. The term *nagid* is used throughout the books of Samuel and Kings in reference to kings Saul, David, Solomon, Jeroboam, Jehu, and Hezekiah. In each case, the term is applied in an instance when the king is either being praised or judged for doing something according to the way of God. For example, even Jeroboam, a northern king, is called a *nagid* and could have had a long rule, much as Saul could have had, if he had followed God's ways (1 Kings 14:7). Likewise, Hezekiah is referred to as a *nagid* at the moment of distress when he relies on God and prays for healing and deliverance (2 Kings 20:5).

One thing that makes a good leader in these passages is a person who listens to God as well as to the people, who lives in covenant with the people and does not lord power over them. It is precisely when leaders rely on their own wisdom, their own strength, and their own ability to accomplish things that they get into trouble. For example, when David trusts God and lives into the covenant God has made with him, David's leadership opens up possibilities for Israel to flourish. It is precisely when David acts as a shepherd and takes care of the people that things go better than when David attempts to live within his own power and wisdom.

As we think about our own way of leading, it might do us well to think about the type of metaphor or model we use to frame leadership. Do we expect leaders to be all-everything (all-powerful, all-knowing, etc.)? Or do we expect them to be shepherds who are compassionate and consider the well-being of those in their care? I believe the text endorses the latter model, and I believe that Christian discipleship shapes us toward that way of being.

A final takeaway is the uncontrollable nature of God. In 2 Samuel 7, David wants to build a house for God partly because he wants to control God's residence and seeks to control God's blessing. God in turn rejects David's request and instead reminds David of all God has done. God then chooses to build a house for David and chooses who will build a house for God's name. This house will not be a place for God to reside but a place for people to honor God's name through right worship. It is important for us to remember that we are not God. This may seem an obvious statement, but I believe all too often we play the role of David in this text and attempt to bend God to our wishes. In such cases it is important to remind ourselves that although God will respond to our hopes and desires, God is also the one who freely moves and works among and with us for good. We do not control God, and attempts to do so do not work out well. When we get the order of things wrong, we often find that even our best efforts come up short.

As the Israelites told their story, one of the things they recognized was how often they failed to work in coordination with God to continue to fulfill God's purposes in the world through the monarchy and the promised land. Unfortunately, they found that they often acted in ways contrary to God's purposes and ended up making things difficult for themselves and others. Wesleyans call this way of living sin—living in ways contrary to the loving purposes of God. When we think we can control God and force God into our way of living, we have missed the point of our purpose in this world. Instead, one of the primary things we can learn from this passage and Israel's history is how to work in a proper relationship with God and trust in God's uncontrollable love. God's work in our lives may be much bigger and better than we can imagine if we will trust in God's ways.

What God offered David in this passage was a relationship of trust. When we live in trust with God, we are able to coordinate our lives according to God's desire to see the world blessed and for *shalom* (the place of wholeness and well-being) to develop in our communities as God has always desired. For this reason, Christian readers of Scripture have pointed to Jesus as the one who finally sits on David's throne. For Jesus's reign is one of eternal peace and well-being founded upon God's rule of love and servant shepherding.

Reflection

Conveyed in 2 Samuel 7:1-17 is the Old Testament theme of God's ongoing presence in the covenant community and the world, past, present, and future. As you reflect on these themes, consider the following:

1. We live in a relationship with a God who reaches out to make and keep covenants with humans. This should give us hope. How have you seen God reach out to you and others in order to foster relationships of covenantal trust?

2. In covenantal relationships, the goal is to bring about well-being in the world. How have you seen God bring about well-being in the world? How have you been called to bring well-being into the world?

3. This text offers us a lens through which to read the rest of the Old Testament: from Abraham and Sarah through the kings of Israel, all of Israel's story can be understood as one of covenantal relationship with God. How might understanding covenant—and especially God's covenant with David—help as a framework for reading the rest of the Old Testament?

7
PSALM 13:1
Christina Bohn

How long, LORD? Will you forget me forever?
How long will you hide your face from me?
—Psalm 13:1, NIV

A few years ago, I was deeply betrayed by several different men who abused their positions of power, leaving me hurt and confused. After a few sessions in counseling, my therapist finally remarked, "Christina, I think that you need to get angry. You are not going to be able to heal until you tap down into the rage hidden deep inside you." Those words were a turning point in my healing. I was comfortable with expressing my grief through tears; crying tends to be my default reaction to pain. But anger? Reacting with anger filled me with guilt. Somehow I had internalized a belief that anger was not a proper "Christian" emotion. Becoming enraged over the pain and injustices inflicted on other people was acceptable; after all, we do see this divine, righteous sort of anger in Jesus, particularly when he confronted the temple authorities. But anger at my own pain? For some reason, that seemed far less acceptable. I was so uncomfortable with vocalizing anger over my pain that the very thought of expressing it in the privacy of my mind made me feel guilty!

Not knowing where else to turn, I opened the book of Psalms. Reading prayers inspired by God that expressed the full range of human emotion gave me the language I did not realize I needed. Through the words of the psalmist in Psalm 13, I was able to express my pain, my sorrow, and even my rage. Several prayers called imprecatory psalms, psalms that ask for judgment against enemies, particularly gave me permission to meet God in a place of unbridled rage.[1] If these prayers were included in our biblical canon as words inspired by God, there was no shame in me adopting these words and postures as my own. Reading these psalms became an exercise in examining my own theology. Did I pray to the God I professed to believe in? If I believed God was the incarnate God who entered into my pain and suffering with me, if I believed that God could handle the full range of my emotions, then why wasn't I encountering this very God within the context of prayer? Did I love God enough to share everything I was thinking and feeling? Did I trust God would still love me? Through the process of praying what are known as the lament psalms, I realized my praying was selective. I was only praying what I thought God could handle. The lament tradition completely challenged my ways of relating to God!

Psalm 13:1 in the Old Testament

Both the Old Testament covenant community and the New Testament church had a rich psalmic heritage. The book of Psalms was the prayer book—and often hymnbook—for both individual and corporate worship in the life of God's people. Encased in this psalmic heritage was a prominent lament tradition that shaped the dialogue these covenantal communities had with God. Roughly 40 percent of the prayers in the book of Psalms are laments. Lament is the biblical response to the reality of suffering in the world. It is a dialogue that engages God in the context of our pain and asks God to respond. Of the lament psalms, the majority are imprecatory (angry/curse) psalms. We see this same kind of sorrowful and

---

1. Psalm 109 became my favorite.

angry dialogue with God in many of the Prophetic Books (such as Jeremiah and Habakkuk) and in Lamentations.

In my experience, the prominence of lament in the Old Testament is often surprising to modern readers; lament does not often make up 40 percent of our own prayers or worship. Yet since the Israelites were in a covenantal relationship with God, they understood the importance of remaining honest with God. In fact, the book of Psalms became a means of faithfulness and commitment to the Israelites' relationship with God in their context of exile. Clearly, we would expect to find prayers of sorrow during Israel's long period of darkness and desolation! These laments oriented the Israelites during their time of disorientation spiritually, emotionally, and even physically. Lament gave the Israelites the language they needed to express their response to trauma, which in turn verified the depth of their relationship with God.

Lament can teach us how to be present to our own
darkness, how to sit in the depth of our pain and sorrow
so that we can find God's presence and healing.

The practice of lament significantly shaped God's people, as is evidenced through its prominence in the Old Testament. Perhaps, in the same way, lament can be a gift to God's people today. To those who do not know how to cry or vent their rage, the wisdom of sorrow and grief may seem foreign. Lament can teach us how to be present to our own darkness, how to sit in the depth of our pain and sorrow so that we can find God's presence and healing. In our periods of exile and alienation from God's presence, lament can be a tool to reorient us to God's presence. God invites our lament.

The lament tradition in the Old Testament also reminds us that we worship a God who shares in our suffering. God has always been the God who sees, hears, and comes down to enter into the pain of his people. Jesus, the incarnate Godhead, who was abandoned by his closest friends and publicly shamed by his enemies, is the ultimate grief bearer. In his greatest moment of pain and alienation from God, Jesus called upon Psalm 22 to give words to his immense suffering: "My God, my God, why have you forsaken me?" (v. 1, NIV). God's Son could have uttered words original to himself, and yet he borrowed a lament from the Old Testament tradition. Jesus, shaped by the Old Testament's tradition of lament, demonstrates to us a God who enters into our human pain.

Psalm 13

In order to demonstrate the centrality of lament in the Old Testament, we will examine Psalm 13 as a case study. Psalm 13 is a short prayer that contains all the traditional features of lament (address, complaint, petition, trust-praise). While many lament psalms contain all these elements, not all laments follow this rubric. Psalm 88, for example, does not transition to trust-praise at its conclusion. Nevertheless, we will examine Psalm 13 as a standard by which we can understand the function of lament in the Old Testament tradition. Psalm 13 also operates as a rubric with which to compare other laments. Psalms that do not follow this format often communicate special meaning through their departure from the standard.

Throughout our examination of Psalm 13, there will be several opportunities for you as the reader to pause for a time of reflection and prayer.[2] It may be tempting to move quickly through the psalm in order to arrive at the "happy" resolution at the end. But instead of rushing to the conclusion, take your time with each step. Lament psalms are designed to walk us through steps of grief; there is intentionality to this process. Since the portion containing hope occurs at the end of the psalm (vv. 5-6), we cannot just read

---

2. See the "Response" section at the close of this chapter.

verse 1 and then skip to the conclusion. It is only by working through the entire psalm, and thus working through all our emotions, that we can find healing. Only by expressing the sum of our entire human experience can we move from lament to praise, from despair to trust.

The Address: Psalm 13:1

"How long, LORD? Will you forget me forever? How long will you hide your face from me?" (v. 1, NIV). David begins by acknowledging the sense of God's absence. As contradictory as it seems, David addresses God, the one who appears missing. Notice that the opening address is to "LORD," a word that in Hebrew refers to *YHWH*, the personal name for God.[3] The chosen name for God is in itself a sign of trust, an entreaty for YHWH to come near and to hear. David still holds on to his intimacy with God and acknowledges the hierarchy of their relationship. Since God feels far away, David entreats God's attention. The contact with God implies David's relationship with God matters. Despite any evidence to the contrary, David is committed to God and hopes God will now turn his face and look at him (see v. 3).

The question "How long?" indicates a desperate sense of urgency for God to become attentive to David. This is not a logical question requesting information, as though revealing a specific measurement of time would soothe David's grief. The question is in itself a form of protest. The question is an announcement that all is not right in God's world; it is a critique of God's inaction. In other words, David is saying, "It's been long enough! I demand you put a stop to this waiting!" In a bold move, the writer reminds God that God is supposed to act as part of the expectations concerning their covenantal relationship.

In the laments in the Old Testament, the most frequently occurring question is *why*, an accusation of unfairness. Psalm 44:23 asks why God appears to be sleeping. Psalm 42:9 asks God why God allows David's ene-

---

3. *YHWH* is the personal name for God, as revealed to Moses in Exodus 3:14. For more on the divine name, please see Michael VanZant's chapter, "Exodus 3:7."

mies to oppress him. All of these questions are rhetorical; David does not expect (or want) a logical, carefully constructed explanation. David wants God to understand the unfairness of the situation. The question communicates a deep desire for God to enter into the pain of God's people. At its core, the biblical practice of lament is criticism, because grief is a signal that all is not right in the world.

The question "How long?" is repeated in 13:1-2 as many times as it appears in the entire rest of the Old Testament.[4] This question contains the Hebrew word for "groan" and conveys a sense of anguish over having to groan or mourn for longer than necessary. The repetition of this question communicates the unfairness of the situation: David is weary of groaning and lamenting. Whenever there is repetition in the Old Testament, it is an attempt to call attention to things God's people often want to forget. The repetition of "How long?" draws our attention to our discomfort with God's inactivity. It reminds us four times in verses 1-2 that we are mourning and groaning, uncomfortable postures and actions we may want to conveniently forget.

David may not have forgotten his own deep pain, but he does accuse God of forgetting. According to David, God has forgotten him and is hiding God's face from him. Psalm 10:1 asks a similar question, wondering why God especially seems absent during times of distress. These accusations are illogical, as both David and the reader know God cannot forget. In the Old Testament, forgetting conveys much more than absent-mindedness. Forgetting is the willful disregard of God's law, the purposeful neglect of keeping the covenant. To accuse God of this same kind of purposeful disregard communicates the depth of David's pain. David knows that God is not prone to forget, and yet it feels as though God has intentionally turned away from him. He is worried that his pain is inconsequential to God. By accusing God of forgetting, David is expressing just how desperately he wants to be seen by God. To an exiled people who felt

---

4. This particular question construct also appears in Habakkuk 1:2 and Job 8:2; 18:2; 19:2.

alienated from God's presence, this kind of bold questioning would have been liberating. Their questions and accusations did not place their relationship with God in jeopardy but became the means by which to regain a reassuring sense of God's presence.

The Complaint: Psalm 13:2

"How long must I wrestle with my thoughts and day after day have sorrow in my heart? How long will my enemy triumph over me?" (v. 2, NIV). After opening the channel of communication with God in verse 1, David voices several complaints. The complaint section is typically the largest portion of the lament. In it the lamenter presents his distress before God in hopes that it will provoke God to act on the lamenter's behalf. The complaint language is usually very evocative because the lamenter is attempting to convince God of the severity of the suffering. In Psalm 13, David recognizes two sources of contention in his life. Internally, the lamenter sees no end in sight to his troubled thoughts and emotions. Externally, the lamenter pleads for a reprieve from his enemies. Both of these enemies are challenges to *shalom*, the biblical concept concerning the flourishing wholeness of God's order. Since these internal and external enemies are opposed to God's order, they are God's enemies too.

Yet Psalm 13 is elusive about the circumstances surrounding these two threats. This ambiguity is one of the beautiful nuances of the psalms. The stylized language permits readers to see themselves in the prayer and to adopt the language as their own. The psalm's description of suffering can be particularized to our own forms of suffering in many different times and circumstances. The enemy language can also prompt readers to participate in the pain of other people. We may not be able to relate to either the internal or external enemies every time we read Psalm 13. The complaints of sickness (Ps. 38) or fear of death (Ps. 55) may not be current threats to our well-being. These laments, however, can help us name social evils that threaten people in our communities. They can connect us to the pain of our neighbors and guide us to pray for their deliverance into shalom. Reading the enemy language in this way invites us into a prayerful imagination where we stand in solidarity with those who suffer in ways we personally do not.

Some of the enemy language in the book of Psalms is startling to modern readers. Occasionally, a psalm cries out for God to inflict violence against the foes. This bloodthirsty language can be particularly disturbing. Psalm 137, for instance, asks God to pay the Babylonians back by inflicting violence against their "little ones" (v. 9, KJV). Psalm 109 expresses a desire for an enemy to lose all he has, including his life. The enemy language in the book of Psalms demonstrates that no emotion or thought is off-limits—not even the angry, vengeful desires we may have against our oppressors. Recognizing that we have enemies, whether they be internal thought patterns, external people, or social structures, is an act of honesty. The angry language is a testament to just how difficult it is for even God's people to love their enemies. The rage, while shocking, demonstrates that the process of learning to love others begins with our acknowledgment of hate. We cannot learn to love our enemies if we are in denial about how we feel about them; honesty about our hatred puts us in a position whereby the God of love can slowly move our hearts to compassion. Ultimately, David leaves his vindication from his oppressors in the hands of God. He expresses what he wants while understanding judgment belongs in God's realm.

By engaging God with our complaints, we are remaining committed to our relationship with God.

During a discussion in one of my Old Testament classes, one of my students asked the poignant question about whether lament was an appropriate "Christian" response because it contained complaining. "How does lament embody the fruit of the Spirit?" the student asked. Perhaps it is best to think of lament as an act of faithfulness, one of Paul's examples of the fruit of the Spirit in Galatians 5:22-23. By engaging God with our complaints, we are remaining committed to our relationship with God. Perhaps choosing not to complain is truly the "unchristian" response: avoiding or ignoring our pain breeds dishonesty and inauthenticity, two characteristics that are antithetical to a healthy, flourishing relationship. Meeting God in the fullness of our humanity is an act of faithfulness for us as God's people. The language of complaint teaches God's people how to speak the truth about our collective human experience.

The Petition: Psalm 13:3-4

"Look on me and answer, LORD my God. Give light to my eyes, or I will sleep in death, and my enemy will say, 'I have overcome him,' and my foes will rejoice when I fall" (vv. 3-4, NIV). Beginning in verse 3, David lists a series of imperatives (commands), audaciously telling God how God is expected to act. David is also implicitly accusing God of being ungod-like; God is not currently doing what God is expected to do, and David is holding God accountable. David recalls what God has done in the past as an appeal for God's consistency. In this way, David is calling into question some traditional beliefs about God. David believes that God is a God of justice (Exod. 34:6-7), and yet the presence of his enemies says otherwise. David believes that God hears the cries of the oppressed (3:7-10), and yet his prayer remains unanswered. Instead of abandoning his beliefs, the lamenter brings these beliefs before God for examination. Is the God to whom he prays consistent with David's theology?

Psalm 44 illustrates the process of questioning deeply held beliefs about God. It begins by recounting what God has done for the Israelites' ancestors. God previously fought their battles because God loved them (v. 3). Yet, despite the people's trust in God and faithfulness to the covenant (vv. 6, 17), God is now no longer protecting God's people (vv. 9-16). This communal lament protests that this is not fair and asks God to wake up from his sleep (vv. 23-24). God is not acting according to God's standards, so the people remind God to show them God's unfailing love once more

(v. 26). Psalm 44, like most laments, is left unresolved. The lament invites us as readers to enter into this tension and ask these same questions.

Other psalms question the Israelites' Zion tradition, the belief that God would always protect the temple, God's dwelling place. This belief was put to the test when the Israelites' enemies destroyed the Temple Mount (2 Kings 25). Psalm 79 views the destruction of the temple as a signal of God's rejection of God's people and petitions God for deliverance. Similarly, Psalm 74 accuses God of passivity as the Israelites' enemies make a mockery of both God and God's people. "Rise up, O God," the psalm pleads, "and defend your cause" (v. 22, NIV).

The petition typically gives specific reasons why God should act on David's behalf. Sometimes the lament lists consequences that will occur if God fails to act. In Psalm 13, the lamenter will "sleep in death" and his enemies will triumph over his defeat (vv. 3-4, NIV). Other times lament psalms petition God for forgiveness of sin, such as in Psalm 51, and demonstrate the extent of David's repentance. Psalm 79:12-13 asks God for retribution against the people's enemies and promises to praise God in response. Psalm 38:17-22 calls upon God for deliverance and appeals to God's relationship with David as a reason for God's swift response. David reminds God that the one who laments matters to God.

During one particularly challenging period of my life, I knew I needed God to intervene, and this sense of needing to hear from God on that day—right then—was urgent. I had deep longings that were unmet, questions that seemed to have no answers, and hurts that could not be healed by anything on this earth. I barricaded myself in my bedroom one day, threw myself before God, and told God that I was not leaving until I received a response. As I remembered the ways in which God had delivered me in my past, my prayer became, "Do it again." I prayed those three words repeatedly during the next few months, appealing to God to act according to what I believed about God's character. The lament tradition shows us that we can tell God to "do it again." We can expect God to act according to how God has revealed God's self to us. Because of the relationship we have with God, we can go before God in prayer with boldness and hold God to God's faithfulness (Heb. 4:16). The God who has been faithful in the past will continue to be faithful to us in the present.

The Response of Trust-Praise: Psalm 13:5-6

"But I trust in your unfailing love; my heart rejoices in your salvation. I will sing the LORD's praise, for he has been good to me" (vv. 5-6, NIV). The "but" signals a shift in the lament. Only after expressing his deep pain and protest does the lamenter transition to a response of trust and praise. David remembers how God has come in the past so that he can trust that God will come again in the future. It is this memory that leads David to hope. Notice that in Psalm 13 none of David's circumstances have changed; David is still awaiting God's intervention. Nevertheless, the lamenter has hope when moving into the future. Because of God's unfailing love, David can trust that God will be good to him once more. Evoking the lament tradition, Micah 7:7 confesses trust in God despite the dire circumstances described immediately before in verses 1-6. Here the prophet waits in hope even though his situation remains the same.

Following the destruction of Jerusalem, the author of Lamentations recalls God's faithfulness. "Because of the LORD's great love we are not consumed," the lamenter reflects (Lam. 3:22, NIV). Nevertheless, this expression of hope is encased within the pain expressed throughout Lamentations 1–5. There is always a tension within the lament tradition between complaint and praise. Many times we as readers focus so much on the praise section of a lament that we, in essence, transform a lament psalm into a thanksgiving psalm. But laments masterfully hold tight to the paradox of grief and thanksgiving, demonstrating to us as readers how to sit in this tension without resolving the two opposing emotions.

As counterintuitive as it seems, lament can help move us into a posture of praise. Expressing our grief, fear, sorrow, and rage can guide us into the praise of the one who enters into our pain with us. The entire structure of the book of Psalms seems to illustrate this movement from lament to praise. The first half of the book (Pss. 1–89) contains more laments; this ratio shifts in the second half (Pss. 90–150) to more hymns of praise. In fact, even though the last portion of the book focuses on Israel's exile experience (Pss. 107–50), the songs make up a grand finale of praise celebrating God's faithfulness! The book of Psalms shows us that disorienting psalms can ultimately reorient us to God's presence.

Yet the book of Psalms also reveals the human struggle of moving from a place of lament to a place of praise. Usually the smallest portion of a lament is the praise section, and not all laments even contain praise. Psalm 88, for instance, has no shift from lament to praise. Instead, the psalm only cycles through complaint, accusation, and petition. Despite its lack of praise and thanksgiving, Psalm 88 is nevertheless inspired by God. It illustrates a posture of refusing to give up on God even when David has no praise to give. This steadfast resolve demonstrates an intimate, resilient relationship with God. Psalm 88 is not the prayer of one who is faithless; it is the prayer of one who possesses a deep, abiding faith.

Sometimes our lament naturally flows into an expression of trust and praise. Other times, we may not be ready to cross over from the one to the other. Perhaps as we are reading Psalm 13, we must pause at verse 4 for a while before continuing to verses 5-6. The psalm does not reveal to us how long it took the writer to move between these two different postures. There are no time stamps that dictate to us as readers how long it should take for us to process our grief in order to move into a position of praise. The movement from lament to praise must not be rushed; we cannot speed the process.

During the seasons when I have turned to lament, I have realized my need to pray the trust parts of the prayer even when I am not ready to profess that same kind of trust. Sometimes I may not believe the words, yet I pray them anyway. Often, praying the words of praise from other people can change us. We may not be in a posture of praise, but we can borrow their language for thanksgiving in the meantime. Imitating David's words and posture can eventually lead to belief if we only keep showing up.

Conclusion

The prominence of lament in the Old Testament reveals a people who were constantly questioning and struggling with their relationship with God. The psalmists struggled with God's goodness and at times wondered whether God was even listening. The prophets struggled with God's justice and lamented over the presence of evil in their world. The exiles struggled with God's promises and questioned whether God would redeem them. In fact, the Israelites' very identity as God's people is one of struggle. Their namesake comes from the story of Jacob's name change to "Israel" after he wrestled with God (Gen. 32:22-32). "Israel" means "one who struggles with God," formally constituting their identity as a people group who were constantly locked in battle with God. Lament gave the Israelites the language whereby to stay in this ongoing battle. Like Jacob, the Israelites intended to hold on to God so they could one day receive God's blessings. By lamenting, the Israelites were determined to stay in their struggle with God for as long as it took; not even exile would dissuade them from remaining faithful.

The Old Testament's lament tradition beautifully shows us how dialogue about pain and sorrow is a way of remaining committed to our relationship with God. It is a means by which we can cultivate intimacy with God. Since pretense has no place in our communication with God, we need not suppress our overwhelming emotions or questions. The Israelites' commitment to lament during their times of great tragedy and suffering gives us the courage to hope today. We do not grieve because there is no hope (1 Thess. 4:13). Rather, God's people grieve because there *is* hope. Our grief is expressed in dialogue with the one who can make all things right. Giving voice to our pain and suffering indicates to God that we are still locked in battle, committed and faithful. According to Romans 8:18-27, all of creation laments, awaiting liberation from pain and suffering.[5] Lament is a practice embedded in the very fabric of the created

---

5. See also Hosea 4:1-3.

order. The Israelites joined their voices with that of creation, and when we evoke the Old Testament tradition of lament today, we join with the entire cosmos in hopefully anticipating God's intervention to bring newness and restoration to this world.

Reflection

Psalm 13 conveys the Old Testament themes of the character and life of the covenant community, drawing together worship and human life and experience in the world. Use Psalm 13 as a guide for prayer. Pause after each section and compose your own lament using the prompts below. As you work through Psalm 13, may this God-inspired prayer invite you to embrace the full emotional range of dialogue with God.

1. Address: What is a name for God that suitably expresses your relationship with God? What questions do you want to ask God? Remember that the questions do not need to be logical; your questions can be rhetorical or even a form of protest.

2. Complaint: What have been the patterns of your thoughts and emotions lately? What has been troubling you? What thought has repeatedly resurfaced? Who or what do you currently see as an "enemy"? What would you like to tell God about your internal and external enemies?

3. Petition: How would you like God to intervene? What do you think God should be expected to do? Trusting in the God who loves you, list a few beliefs you have about God and give God reasons why you expect God to act based on God's faithfulness in the past.

4. Trust-Praise: If you are ready to move into a response of trust and praise, recount how God has been good to you. With what can your heart rejoice? If you are not ready to move into a response of trust and praise, try praying David's response in Psalm 13, even if your heart does not believe it yet. Resolve to remain committed in the tension.

8
PROVERBS 1:7
Timothy M. Green

> *The fear of the LORD is the beginning of knowledge;*
> *fools despise wisdom and instruction.*
> —Proverbs 1:7, NRSV

Proverbs 1:7 in the Old Testament

When thinking of the various voices within the Old Testament, the image of a mass choir often comes to my mind. Just as the diverse voices produce a harmony that complements the melody sung by the full choir, so do the many voices within the Old Testament beautifully enhance the unfolding story of God's engagement with the world. Amid these many voices, however, there is an essential and consistent voice that all too easily becomes muted, even silenced. It is the voice of wisdom. While the Wisdom Books of the Old Testament are often identified as Proverbs, Job, and Ecclesiastes, the tentacles of wisdom thought and language spread wide and deep throughout the Old Testament.

Why the voice of wisdom often seems muted is something we can only imagine. Perhaps some of the underlying thoughts and convictions of wisdom, while not contradictory to the rest of the Old Testament, appear to be quite different or even out of place. It may be that most of the other materials seem to fit nicely into a familiar story line from creation to promise, deliverance to law, judges to monarchy, and, finally, exile to return. Since the traditional Wisdom Books do not seem to fit neatly into that plot, we may ignore them altogether. Refusing to be shoved into a specific segment of a time line, wisdom is timeless. It is less a story that fits with other stories and more a way of thinking about God as creator and about human beings in relationship to God's created order. Richard Clifford observes that when Old Testament wisdom is viewed as a "foreign body" to Scripture, we have likely already made an interpretative conclusion "based on the assumption that the historical and prophetic books are normative for what is genuinely biblical."[1] As a result, the voice of wisdom may become muted or abandoned altogether.

As we hear wisdom's call, we are likely to discover that
we have come face-to-face with a long-lost friend.

Even if it may seem at first that wisdom offers the Old Testament choir nothing but dissonance, wisdom keeps singing its part as it calls, shapes, and guides readers who will listen to its voice. The challenge that we face is not so much to bring wisdom back to the Bible. Wisdom never left the Bible! Our challenge is to allow this voice to be unmuted to sing not merely a periodic solo in a diminished whisper but with the biblical choir in full voice. As we hear wisdom's call, we are likely to discover that we have come face-to-face with a long-lost friend or that we have encountered a brand-new friend in Scripture. The most appropriate place for us to hear this call initially is in the opening purpose statement and thesis in Proverbs 1:2-7.

---

1. Richard J. Clifford, "Introduction to Wisdom Literature," in *The New Interpreter's Bible* (Nashville: Abingdon Press, 1997), 5:2.

Encountered by Wisdom's Motto and Purpose: Proverbs 1:2-7

There are perhaps no more hospitable words spoken at the outset of a journey than, "We'll leave the porch light on for you." There is something about that light on the front porch that says, "Come on in! We're home, and we've been waiting for you." As we enter the unique world of wisdom, that welcoming light burns brightly in the opening verses of Proverbs. These verses open the door not only to the book itself but also to the convictions and thoughts of wisdom generally. Subsequent to the opening editorial comment about ancient Israel's patron king of wisdom, Solomon (see 1 Kings 3:5-15), these six verses provide a statement about wisdom's purpose (Prov. 1:2-6) and the thesis of Old Testament wisdom (v. 7).

Wisdom's Thesis: Proverbs 1:7

Although it appears in the final verse of this introductory passage, the thesis statement in verse 7 provides the context within which all of wisdom is to be understood and practiced: "The fear of YHWH is the beginning of knowledge; fools despise wisdom and discipline." In this almost motto-like statement, the emphasis is not first upon wisdom itself or upon the acquisition of knowledge and discipline. Rather, the central conviction of biblical wisdom is articulated in a concise two-word (in Hebrew) phrase: "[the] fear [of] YHWH." The same thought is echoed toward the end of the first major section of the book of Proverbs: "The beginning of wisdom is the fear of YHWH; knowledge of the Holy One is understanding" (9:10). Likewise, it appears at the conclusion of the book: "A woman who fears YHWH is to be praised" (31:30). From beginning to end, the concept of "the fear of YHWH" is interwoven over a dozen times in Proverbs. With this brief phrase, all that will be said and done is placed within a distinct contextual framework. While Old Testament wisdom shares various similarities with Egyptian and Mesopotamian wisdom, this simple yet profound phrase provides biblical wisdom its distinct context that is obviously not found in neighboring cultures.

Because the meaning of this phrase could easily be misconstrued, it is significant for us to understand how our biblical ancestors perceived this notion. They would certainly not have viewed it in the sense of being terrorized or overcome with anxiety, distress, and panic in the presence of the Lord. Rather, this phrase denotes the acknowledgment that YHWH is the covenant God of the covenant people Israel. It likewise acknowledges that YHWH is the maker of heaven and earth and thus the creator of the order within creation. These acknowledgments in turn evoke the people's response of reverence for, worship of, and faithful service to the Lord. A similar commitment underlies the prophetic-Deuteronomic call for the people's wholehearted loyalty to YHWH (e.g., Deut. 6:4-5, 13; 10:20; Josh. 24:14) as well as the priestly call for the people to be holy because YHWH is holy (Lev. 19:2).

The intentional use of God's name, YHWH, in this phrase is essential to biblical wisdom's thesis. The context within which wisdom occurs is not reverence for, worship of, or service to whatever ancient Near Eastern deity one may desire. Rather, the entry point into the thought of biblical wisdom is the reverent worship of and service to ancient Israel's distinct covenant God, YHWH. In the minds of our biblical ancestors, that name conjures up memories of and testimonies to YHWH's mighty acts of promise to the ancestors: the deliverance from Egyptian captivity, provision in the wilderness, the covenant at Sinai, and guidance into the land. While Old Testament wisdom does not make specific reference to these central moments in the life of the people of the Lord, wisdom's thesis—the fear of YHWH—rests upon the unique identity of the God who acted on behalf of our biblical ancestors. Terence Fretheim reminds us that "while Israel's particular story is of no apparent interest to the earlier wisdom teachers and writers, Israel's God is basic to their reflections."[2] Through this two-word phrase, wisdom finds its home within the life of God's covenant people so that wisdom can declare, "YHWH gives wisdom, from his mouth come knowledge and understanding" (Prov. 2:6).

---

2. Terence E. Fretheim, *God and World in the Old Testament: A Relational Theology of Creation* (Nashville: Abingdon Press, 2005), 200.

Recalling the first word of the Bible, "beginning" (Gen. 1:1), biblical wisdom's thesis statement describes the starting point for all wisdom. Reverence for the Lord provides not only the context for wisdom but also the impetus for wisdom. Roland Murphy insightfully observes that "it is surely remarkable that a commitment to God lies at the basis of the wisdom enterprise."[3]

While biblical wisdom is certainly viewed as a human exercise that involves close observation and subsequent action, it is first viewed as God's gracious gift that precedes all human activity. Describing the synergistic relationship between the divine gift of wisdom and humanity's "discovery" of wisdom, James Crenshaw recounts the story of a little girl who became lost in the woods. Fearful and exhausted, she fell asleep beside a log. In the meantime, her parents set out to search for her. Finding her asleep, her father inadvertently "stepped on some dry twigs that snapped explosively, awaking her. Seeing her father, the girl cried out, 'Daddy, I've found you.'"[4] Applying the story to humanity's search for wisdom, Crenshaw observes that "Israel's wise men and women searched diligently too, but in the end became the willing objects of a greater pursuit. The search became truly Royal, one in which God came in search of humans."[5]

While our Old Testament ancestors were keenly aware that wisdom is the gracious gift of God, they were also profoundly conscious of humanity's perpetual dilemma of exchanging the wisdom of the Creator for the creature's own wisdom. As a result of this exchange, humanity seeks to determine in its own eyes what is good (life giving) and what is evil (life taking). Leaning outside of wisdom's starting point of the fear of the Lord, humanity became wise in its own eyes, viewing God's *good* as *evil* and God's *evil* as *good*. Similar thought is echoed in the prophetic words

---

3. Roland E. Murphy, *The Tree of Life: An Exploration of Biblical Wisdom Literature* (Grand Rapids: Eerdmans, 1990), 16.

4. James L. Crenshaw, *Old Testament Wisdom: An Introduction* (Atlanta: John Knox Press, 1981), 64.

5. Ibid.

of Isaiah: "Ah, you who call evil good and good evil, who put darkness for light and light for darkness, who put bitter for sweet and sweet for bitter! Ah, you who are wise in your own eyes, and shrewd in your own sight" (Isa. 5:20-21, NRSV). Indeed, the voice of wisdom runs parallel with the prophetic voice: "Trust in YHWH with all your heart, and do not lean on your own understanding. In all your ways, know him, and he will make your paths straight. Do not be wise in your eyes; revere YHWH, and turn around from evil" (Prov. 3:5-7).

Certainly the easy way out for our biblical ancestors would have been to conclude that their only resolution to this dilemma is the avoidance of wisdom with its accompanying knowledge, instruction, and discernment. One might even ask, "Would it not be best simply to run away from wisdom altogether?" The voice of biblical wisdom responds with a resounding, "By no means!" Biblical wisdom refuses a simplistic escapism. Wisdom is the gift of God! Why would any human being consider rejecting God's gracious gift of wisdom, knowledge, instruction, and discernment? Therefore, wisdom never ceases to call out, "Get wisdom, . . . and the beginning of wisdom is reverence for, worship of, and service to the LORD!"

Beyond its emphasis upon the "fear of the LORD," the thesis statement in 1:7 introduces three interrelated words that recur throughout Proverbs: knowledge (*da'at*), wisdom (*hokhmah*), and instruction (*musar*). Appearing in this same order at the opening of our passage in verse 2, these words provide a frame around the full passage. Within the wisdom tradition, *da'at* generally indicates what is acquired through the act of learning (i.e., knowledge). While such learning certainly included *information*, that information served the greater end of the *formation* of persons so that significant "life skills" might appropriately be carried out.

While *musar* is frequently translated as "instruction," the term denotes that type of instruction that involves the necessary correction or discipline for proper learning to occur. Such correction or discipline is by no means for the purpose of shaming, humiliating, or injuring a learner. Instead, it is for the sake of encouraging the learner to mature from false-hood to truthfulness, from error to accuracy.

Between these two words is the word most often translated as wisdom—*hokhmah* In its general sense, this term signifies the skill to carry out a particular task such as working with metals, designing jewelry, constructing ships, making judicial decisions, or even mourning. Richard Clifford has observed that this notion of wisdom is closely related to the French term *savoir-faire*, meaning "'to know how to act or do,' rather than 'to know' in an absolute sense, divorced from action."[6] Wisdom is never merely the acquisition of knowledge for the sake of knowledge per se but rather the acquisition of knowledge for the sake of skillfully (wisely) engaging in life.

Toward the end of verse 7, a familiar character in the biblical world of wisdom appears: the fool. Just as foolishness is the opposite of wisdom, so is the foolish person a foil to the wise person. The wise person embraces wisdom; the fool detests wisdom. While our contemporary culture typically uses this term as a derogatory attack on another person without any consideration of wisdom, biblical wisdom speaks of one as a *fool* only in light of and in contrast to the wise person (see discussion below on the two paths).

Wisdom's Purpose: Proverbs 1:2-6

The five verses preceding the thesis statement in verse 7 provide an overview of the intended outcomes or purposes of wisdom. Describing the abundance of words in these few verses as conveying "the riches of wisdom," Murphy observes that these words "are not abstract, merely intellectual characteristics; they are tied to the practical aspects of human conduct."[7] While it would be appealing to dissect each one, the passage functions as a whole to depict wisdom's bountiful benefits.

The invitation of wisdom extends to all human beings, from the very young and immature (often translated as "simple"; literally "open" or "empty," as in a mind waiting to be filled) who are preparing to set out on

---

6. Clifford, "Wisdom Literature," in *New Interpreter's Bible*, 5:11.

7. Murphy, *Tree of Life*, 16.

the journey to the maturing young adults who have already embarked on the journey (v. 4) to the wise elders whose lifelong journey with wisdom has allowed them to gain knowledge and discernment (v. 5). A consistent benchmark by which the wise life is measured is one's engagement in right relationships with God, humans, and all creation. This commitment to rightly ordered relationality is routinely articulated not only in wisdom but also in the Torah and the Prophets as *righteousness*, *justice*, and *equity* (v. 3).

Wisdom seeks to provide a world in which understanding and knowledge, thoughtful discernment and critical reflection, and disciplined insight and right-related living become the norm.

Old Testament wisdom regularly invites human beings to learn and think about, to reflect on and ask questions concerning, the wise teachings that have been passed down across the generations of wise people through proverbs, parables, sayings, and riddles (v. 6). Ultimately, wisdom seeks to provide a world in which understanding and knowledge, thoughtful discernment and critical reflection, and disciplined insight and right-related living become the norm. Anything otherwise would become life in opposition to the wisdom of God—namely, foolishness.

As the opening verses of Proverbs provide the light on wisdom's front porch, a welcome is given to anyone who is willing to step into this unique world. Crossing the threshold into that world, we hear wisdom's thesis echo clearly: "The fear of the LORD is the beginning . . ."

Entering the World of Wisdom

There is certainly no more appropriate way to enter the biblical world of wisdom than by intentionally, reflectively, and prayerfully reading the books of Proverbs, Job, and Ecclesiastes. However, to prepare for that reading, a general understanding of wisdom's most deeply held convictions is beneficial. These convictions include the synergistic relationship between God's gift of the created order and the God-given human capacity to perceive that order, the two pathways and their ends, wisdom as embodied living, and wisdom's honest self-examination and continuing journey forward.

God's Gift of the Created Order and the God-Given Human Capacity to Perceive That Order

Undergirding the thought world of biblical wisdom is the deeply held conviction that God has created all that exists in an orderly manner so that within God's creation is "a divinely implanted order"[8] that is observable by human beings. Within this rightly ordered creation, God wills that all created beings, human and nonhuman, participate in an intricate web of relationality that includes the Creator, humanity, and all other creatures. Founding the earth and establishing the heavens by divine wisdom, God brings forth wisdom before the earth, the heavens, and the seas ever existed (see Prov. 3:19-20; 8:22-30a). In the magnificent hymn of Proverbs 8, which depicts the joy and wonder over God's creative work, wisdom is portrayed as being God's delight, the master worker who takes joy both in God and in humanity (vv. 30-31).

Refusing to begin with human action, the thought world of wisdom is firmly grounded in God's initiating gracious activity in creation. Nevertheless, a synergistic relationship emerges between God's initiating gracious work of creation and humanity's response. Just as other voices in the Old Testament portray God as entrusting the divine mission in the world

---

8. Clifford, "Wisdom Literature," in *New Interpreter's Bible*, 5:9.

to humanity (e.g., Gen. 1:28-30; 2:15; 12:1-3; Exod. 19:4-6), so, too, does the voice of wisdom believe that God has uniquely created human beings with the divine gift of observing and thoughtfully reflecting upon God's created order in such a way that they might act accordingly.

To live life according to the rightly ordered work of the Creator and thus to be rightly related to God, human beings, and all creation is to be *tsedeq* (often translated as "righteous"). Therefore, to follow the way of wisdom is to follow the path of right-relatedness or "righteousness." There is a direct correlation between biblical wisdom's understanding of faithful living according to God's gift of an ordered creation and the understanding of faithful living according to God's gift of *torah* (instruction) as found throughout much of the Old Testament. Both the Lord's created order and the Lord's *torah* are indeed gifts of God, one to all creation and the other to the covenant community for the sake of all creation. It comes as no surprise that Psalm 19 easily transitions from the celebration of God's orderly creation, which pours forth speech and knowledge (vv. 1-4), to the celebration of God's *torah*, with its decrees, precepts, and commandments that give life to the soul and wisdom to the simpleminded (vv. 7-13). Similarly, the opening psalm of the Psalter is a wisdom song that contrasts the two paths typically offered by wisdom (see below), identifying those persons who are faithful to *torah* as "righteous."

Because God's created order is observable by all humanity and not merely a select few, our biblical ancestors recognized that valuable insights into that order also emerged from observations of wise people outside of their own community and faith. In the description of Solomon's renowned wisdom, the writer acknowledges the notorious wisdom of both Mesopotamian and Egyptian wise people: "The wisdom of Solomon exceeded the wisdom of all persons from the east and all of the wisdom of Egypt. He was wiser than all humans, wiser than Ethan the Ezrahite, and than Heman, Calcol, and Darda, the children of Mahol" (1 Kings 4:30-31).

As the description of Solomon's notorious wisdom continues in verses 32-33, the biblical text provides significant insight into just how deep and broad and wide the wisdom of God's created order really is. For Solomon, the gift of wisdom leads him to compose three thousand proverbs and over a thousand songs. It takes him into conversations about plants and animals of every type. Wisdom leads human beings to observe, to think deeply, to discover and imagine, to ask questions, and to implement what today might be called the natural and social sciences, the arts, the use of words in speech and poetry. Wisdom calls upon humanity to learn from the great tradition of wise insights, sayings, and instruction that have been handed down over the centuries and to engage in them with human reason and collective human experience for the sake of subsequent generations—all in the context of reverence for, worship of, and service to the Lord.

This God-given vocation to participate fully in the Creator's rightly ordered web of relationality is rooted in the Old Testament's understanding of humanity's place within creation (e.g., see Gen. 1–2; Ps. 8). Wisdom views human beings as more than task-driven producers or disposable machine parts. Humanity is the thinking, relational, creative, imaginative, reasoning, expressive image of God that is called to engage fully in and with all of God's creation. Fretheim reminds us that rather than a divine call "to be passive recipients of God-given blessings," this human vocation "implies a strong emphasis on God's expressed confidence in human beings, entrusting them with responsibility to discern the character of the social and natural orders, their interrelationship, and the implications for daily life."[9]

The Two Pathways and Their Ends

Wisdom is by no means merely a collection of knowledge that views knowledge per se as the end goal. Rather, wisdom is a journey to be taken, a pathway to follow, in order to experience life fully as envisioned by the creator of all life. Indeed, wisdom is "a tree of life to the ones who take hold of her" (Prov. 3:18). Old Testament wisdom envisions all human beings standing at a fork in the road with one pathway being wisdom (or righteousness) and the other being foolishness (or wickedness).

---

9. Fretheim, *God and World*, 201.

Often personified as a woman (see Prov. 8–9; 31; see also less-er-known but significant stories of wise women such as Abigail in 1 Sam. 25 and the anonymous wise woman of Tekoa in 2 Sam. 14), wisdom calls upon human beings who stand at the fork in the road to follow her pathway. Her way is one of prudence, knowledge, right-relatedness, instruction, and discretion. Her path avoids evil, pride, arrogance, and perverted speech (Prov. 8:1-4, 6-7a). Ultimately, wisdom's way is the truthfulness that leads to life. Wisdom exclaims, "The one who finds me [finds] life. . . . The ones who hate me love death" (vv. 35a, 36b).

In contrast to wisdom's call, foolishness also stands at the same fork in the road pointing to the way of falsehood that leads to destruction. Depicted as loud, wayward, careless, arrogant, and persuasive, foolishness invites those who lack sense to follow her on the journey all the way down to Sheol, the "chambers of death" (Prov. 7:27, NRSV; see also 9:16-18).

Each of the two pathways has a clear "end" or destination: life or death. No one arbitrarily rewards or punishes the wise with life or the foolish with death. Living in Nashville, if I take the interstate east, I will end in Knoxville; if I take the interstate west, I will end in Memphis. Each road has its destination. Similar to wisdom's two ways, prophetic thought in the Old Testament understands two paths as well: the path of good that leads to life and the path of evil that leads to death (see Deut. 30:15-20). The prophetic call could just as easily emerge from the mouth of wisdom: "Choose life!"

Wisdom as Embodied Living

Wisdom calls upon all who travel its pathway to embody—to put into practice—the wise life in daily, commonplace matters. Likely to have first emerged from family and tribal settings rather than from formal schools, wisdom's instructions "are not the creation of a study desk; they grew out of human situations and needs."[10] Out of common human circumstances, simple, memorable statements and concise, straightforward

---

10. Murphy, *Tree of Life*, 4.

admonitions were faithfully transmitted from one generation to the next. Emerging out of ordinary life and guided by the same Spirit that guided the other voices of the Old Testament, wisdom refuses to separate the body and its actions from some type of spiritualized or religious life that disregards or devalues everyday living. Any notion that divides life into a sacred sphere and a secular sphere could not even be imagined by biblical wisdom. What humans do with their bodies, their words, their relationships, and their daily activities really does matter. Therefore, wisdom is deeply concerned with common-life matters as diverse as temper tantrums, laziness, gossip, gluttony and drunkenness, character formation, pride, sexual passion, jealousy, wise counsel, marriage and raising children, troublemaking, spoken words (and perhaps today typed words), the workplace, and the honorable treatment of the elderly. In other words, wisdom passionately cares about the everyday life that is lived in the real-life, flesh-and-blood, here and now.

Wisdom's Honest Self-Examination and Continuing Journey Forward

Remaining true to its character of observing life honestly, wisdom refuses to calcify its former conclusions into hardened dogma or to accept its own known falsehoods as truthfulness or to settle for the unexamined life. Wisdom boldly asks probing questions not first of others but of itself and of its own predetermined conclusions when the realities of life demonstrate something different. Rather than viewing such self-honesty as weak, intimidating, or threatening, wisdom views any other option than honesty as contradictory to what it seeks—truth.

The writings of Job and Ecclesiastes particularly reveal biblical wisdom's practice of honest self-examination. For the book of Job, wisdom's concept of two paths that lead to distinct outcomes became all too easily applied in a mechanical, formulaic, almost magical manner: "If one does x, one will receive y." As a result, one might take a certain path assured that she or he will reach a specified end, or one might observe the circumstances of another and determine which path that other person has followed. The book of Job dares to disagree vehemently with such a dogmatic understanding. Raising his voice with the honest and sincere lament of grief, dismay, and abandonment that is found in other Old Testament writings such as the Psalms, Lamentations, and Jeremiah, Job boldly curses the day of his birth (Job 3:1-3) and refuses to back down when his friends confront him.

Protesting the apparent breakdown of creation's order that he had previously assumed, Job engages in reasoned yet heated conversation with his wise friends who represent a "popularized" version of the paths of wisdom (see Job 4–37). From their interpretation of the two paths, Job's friends logically conclude that Job has either traveled the path of wickedness and folly or that God is refining Job into a much more righteous person. As Brueggemann observes, their "reflection on experience has been hardened into dogmatic conviction that requires experience to conform to preconceived patterns of morality."[11] In response, wisdom (Job) confronts wisdom (the friends). In the end, God entreats Job to pray and sacrifice on behalf of the wise friends who have spoken foolishly by speaking what is not truthful about God (42:8).

Likewise, the books of Job and Ecclesiastes both ask the looming question that emerges from a hardened dogma of the two paths: Is it even possible for a human to take the path of wisdom-righteousness simply for the sheer joy of wisdom-righteousness and not for the ulterior motive of receiving a greater reward at the end of the path? "Does Job revere God gratuitously [i.e., to get nothing out of it]?" (Job 1:9). "What profit is there for humans in all the toil that they do?" (Eccles. 1:3). What thought-provoking and challenging questions to be asked by a tradition that had consistently spoken of the destination of the path rather than the joy of the path itself! Can one worship God simply for the sake of worshipping God and not for fringe benefits? Can one engage in work simply for the delight of work?

---

11. Walter Brueggemann, *Reverberations of Faith: A Theological Handbook of Old Testament Themes* (Louisville, KY: Westminster John Knox Press, 2002), 234.

As wisdom raised questions of itself and engaged in honest self-examination, it also continued its journey forward beyond the thirty-nine books of our Old Testament. As circumstances changed and new realities emerged, the seed of wisdom continued to sprout new growth. In subsequent wisdom writings prior to the time of Jesus, large segments are devoted to hymns of gratitude to God for the divine wisdom that was evident in the Lord's mighty acts of the exodus and the nourishment in the wilderness (Wis. 10:15–19:22). The lives and wisdom of the faithful heroes of ancient Israel's story are celebrated, from Enoch, Noah, and the ancestors to the judges, rulers, and prophets (Sir. 44–50; Wis. 10:1-14).[12] In these writings, the gift of wisdom in God's ordered creation becomes one and the same as the gift of God's *torah* to ancient Israel (Sir. 24:19-23).

As the early followers of Jesus testified to who he was, they took a further step and confessed that Jesus was the very wisdom of God in flesh and blood. He himself is the *way* of God's *truth* that leads to *life* (John 14:6). As noted by Brueggemann, "Jesus is not only a wisdom teacher, but he is the embodiment of the wisdom of God that provides the coherence and visibility of God's creation."[13] Therefore, confessing Jesus to be the very *wisdom* of God (1 Cor. 1:24), the apostle Paul describes him as the "firstborn of all creation," in whom "all things in heaven and on earth were created . . . all things have been created through him and for him. He himself is before all things, and in him all things hold together" (Col. 1:15-17, NRSV; see also the *word made flesh* in John 1:1-5, 14). No wonder, Jesus calls out with the invitation to *come and learn* from him and find rest for one's weary and burdened soul (Matt. 11:29). Indeed, Jesus describes all who hear and do his words to be like the *wise* person who built a house upon a rock (7:24).

---

12. Sirach (Sir.) and Wisdom of Solomon (Wis.) are books from the Apocrypha.

13. Brueggemann, *Reverberations of Faith*, 234.

Reflection

Proverbs 1:7 reflects the Old Testament theme of human life and experience in the world. Perhaps now is the time or even past time for the biblical voice of wisdom to be "unmuted" so that it can again join— with full voice—in the biblical choir's harmonious melody. Where might we begin in welcoming wisdom back into the choir? May I suggest a few possibilities?

1. Prayerfully design a plan to engage in a careful and intentional reading of the books of Proverbs, Job, and Ecclesiastes. Chew on small bites at a time. Engaging in wisdom is not a sprint; it is a joyful marathon! If possible, participate in a small group whose members are also reading these books and reflectively engaging in conversation.

2. Since "the fear of the LORD" is the essential context of biblical wisdom, intentionally engage in Christian practices and disciplines by which the Holy Spirit will continue to form and mature your reverence for, worship of, and service to God.

3. Wisdom's nature is one of observing, gaining insight, and asking questions about life and creation. With this understanding of wisdom in mind, select a topic of interest (perhaps something in creation, human relationships, the arts, history, etc.) and explore it further.

4. Select an individual who is presently engaged in an area of wisdom (e.g., medicine, education, research, grandparenting, counseling, and the arts), and find a way to express your gratitude for what that person is contributing to life and to future generations.

When all is said and done, by the grace of God, "Get wisdom . . . and the beginning of wisdom is the fear of the LORD!"

9
ISAIAH 53:11
Marty Alan Michelson

> *Out of his anguish he shall see light;*
> *he shall find satisfaction through his knowledge.*
> *The righteous one, my servant, shall make many righteous,*
> *and he shall bear their iniquities*
> —Isaiah 53:11, NRSV

Isaiah 53:11 in the Old Testament

For followers of Jesus, Isaiah is likely the best-known prophet of the Old Testament. Quotes from the book of Isaiah are used throughout the New Testament. The message the Lord revealed to Isaiah, Isaiah proclaimed to the people of God. The announcements from the Lord to Isaiah set the framework for how God's work was already unfolding in the prophet's time and for how God's work would unfold at the time of Jesus and on through to the present.

The passage under consideration here (specifically Isa. 52:13–53:12) comes into view when we consider its broader historical and literary contexts. It appears in a section of the book of Isaiah that has a particular setting. The historical prophet Isaiah, whose words dominate chapters 1–39 of the book, proclaimed God's messages to the Southern Kingdom of Judah in the midst of complex social, political, and religious realities in the mid-eighth century BCE. When the prophet died (sometime after 701 BCE), a group of his followers and associates carried his messages forward into the next era. This group expanded the scope of Isaiah's original messages and added new prophecies that carried on his spirit and became part of the book now known as Isaiah in modern Bibles. These new messages centered on God's revelation in light of the devastating experiences of Jerusalem's destruction and the people's exile at the hands of the Babylonians in 586 BCE.

Many of the Judeans were carried off from Jerusalem to the capital city of their enemies in Babylon. There the people of the Lord and the disciples of Isaiah pondered their failures and attempted to discern how God was acting. The book of Lamentations, for example, reveals that the people were even asking if God's actions were signs that God had cut them off completely (Lam. 5:21-22). It was in this context that the people of God and the disciples of Isaiah continued to read, study, and understand the previous messages of Isaiah. It was here, too, that they discerned anew what Isaiah had announced and how God could still be active, even in the midst of their disruption from Jerusalem. They heard a fresh word from the Lord that gave hope and meaning to their plight, especially about how the Lord might be shaping a future for Judah out of the experiences of suffering, loss, and exile.

A series of prophetic messages in the latter part of the book of Isaiah announce that God's purpose and plan would unfold through one known as the "servant," specifically a servant who has suffered (the Suffering Servant). Isaiah 52:13–53:12 is central to the identity of this Suffering Servant. This passage has also become central to the Christian understanding of Jesus's mission and work. Yet the figure and identity of a servant appears in several passages in Isaiah (the so-called Servant Songs: 42:1-4; 49:1-6; 50:4-9; 52:13–53:12). Each of these passages contributes to a full understanding of God's work through a servant in the midst of Israel's suffering and exile.

For Isaiah 53 in particular, three broader Old Testament themes appear in important and distinctive ways: (1) God's saving work, (2) how

God partners in salvation, and what this means for (3) God's ongoing presence in the covenant community and the world, past, present, and future.

God's Saving Work

The prophetic poem of Isaiah 52:13–53:12 announces the saving work of God in a new way. This is God's "astonishing" (see 52:14, NRSV) and "startling" (see 52:15, NRSV) new revelation. For the people who were the first recipients of this revelation, the message gave new meaning to their experiences of forced deportation and disruption in the Babylonian exile. But this revelation also pointed forward to the redemption that God would achieve in the person and work of Jesus in ways that the exiles could not yet fully understand.

God's way is humble. It does away with pomp and circumstance in favor of self-sacrifice.

Certainly a common assumption among many religious people is that a deity is powerful and mighty. People in the ancient Near East, where Israel and Judah were located, understood their gods to have power over the fruitfulness of the fields, crops, and offspring of their herds. The gods, they believed, had authority over the nation and gave victory to them when they fought battles with their enemies. This same idea, no doubt, was true for Judeans with their belief in God. Judeans and the former inhabitants of Jerusalem had understood that God was responsible for the produce of the fields and, when it came, victory over other nations on the battlefield. The announcements and belief about God's sovereignty appear throughout the Old Testament. They resonate with the depictions of God as a warrior (Exod. 15) who defeated Pharaoh at the sea and as a king in various psalms (Pss. 93–94, 96). In the prophetic poem of Isaiah 52:13–

53:12, however, a new way of perceiving the action of God was emerging in the world! And this was a perception of God that seemingly did not align with the way any of the other nations saw their gods. Here the language of victory and might shifts not only to servant language but also to descriptions of suffering, pain, and death. With the vision of a suffering servant and in Israel's call to embody this way of serving, the prophet hails a new reality.

The prophet's message declares that God will be known in service, even to the point of being rejected as a servant (52:13; 53:3). God works through despised means, choosing "my servant" to accomplish God's work! God's activity among human persons here takes the form not of power or authority, but service. God's way is humble. It does away with pomp and circumstance in favor of self-sacrifice. Although such proclamations may sound familiar to Christians today, in the exile of the people of Judah, this revelation brought something new. Not only had God not been characterized in this way, but also no nations talked about finding victory through sacrifice and suffering.

In the midst of exile, it would have been easy for God's people to believe any variety of claims that their God was dead or that the Babylonian gods were more powerful or that the power of their God could not be awakened on their behalf. They may have been tempted to abandon their God and take up belief in the gods of the nations who conquered them. And yet, for Judah, this was not their new reality. Their new reality was shaped by this word of the Lord given to the prophet that proclaimed that their God would be known in and through the experience of dislocation, exile, and suffering as a God who partnered with and participated in the hurt, turmoil, and brokenness of the world. This God who could "astonish" (see 52:14, NRSV) would become "marred" in appearance such that his form would "startle many nations" and "shut [the] mouths" of kings (vv. 14-15, NRSV). The Lord announces that "my servant shall prosper" (52:13, NRSV; 53:10) even in the state of being marred and condemned.

Let me offer a thought experiment for considering how unparalleled this announcement would have been to its first audience. Two competitors enter a boxing match. A few rounds later, one of them has fallen on the mat, collapsed from exhaustion, eyes swollen and lip bloodied. No reasonable observer would think this person was the victor. Yet in a way not too dissimilar from this, Isaiah 53 announces that Judah has become this servant appointed by God, and this is the way that God will work for and with Judah for its sake and the sake of all people. God's means of salvation will emerge from the servant who is "despised" and of "no account" (v. 3, NRSV).

The servant is not one who is free from disease; instead, God's new way to save will come through the one who takes on "infirmities," is "stricken," is "afflicted," is "wounded for our transgressions," is "crushed," and takes on "our iniquities" (vv. 4-5, NRSV). The beaten body of the one who is crushed rises in God's power as one who is "my servant." If we don't discern this clearly enough in Isaiah's first statements already reviewed (vv. 3-5), verses 6-7 carry on with similar language. The saving work of God will come to pass in humbled subjugation, not domination. The saving work of God will present its force in power precisely by its submission to the forces of the kings who will only "shut their mouths" (52:15, NRSV) in light of this new work of God. The last line of this Servant Song captures the idea most radically: the humiliated servant will have "a portion with the great" and will receive a division of "spoil with the strong" precisely because he "poured out himself to death . . . and made intercession for the transgressors" (53:12, NRSV).

How God Partners in Salvation

In addition to discerning the saving work of God in Isaiah 53, we also discern how God partners with others to achieve God's saving purposes. The full scope of the story of the Old Testament is testimony to a God who needs no partners, since God can create and sustain by God's own might. Yet Scripture testifies that God chooses partners to achieve God's purposes. These are, at times, persons such as Abraham, Sarah, Moses, Miriam, Joshua, and Deborah. At other times, God chooses the people of Israel as a whole to be God's partner (see Exod. 19). The Servant Songs in the book of Isaiah sometimes identify the servant explicitly as Israel (41:8; 44:1-2). In other places, such as in Isaiah 53, the servant seems to be some unidentified representative of the people and their suffering in exile (which led eventually to the later Christian identification of this servant as Jesus). The point is that God's saving work is enacted in the vicarious suffering of human servants.

Here we see that God's partnership with Israel is not simply for its own sake or because Israel was special prior to God's choosing. In fact, in God's choice of Israel God announces something declarative about God's choice of partners for his redemptive work in the world—namely, that God chooses the weak, lowly, and few (Deut. 7:7-8 makes this explicit). The Judeans were despised and debased in the exile and may have even felt cut off from God (see Isa. 40:27). But to the very people who experienced the chastisement of the Babylonians, God announces through the prophet that this is how God achieves God's work in the world.

Christian readers see this divine practice as most fully realized in the daily life that Jesus models in the New Testament Gospels. Israel is God's servant, and Jesus is God's servant. And those who follow in the way of suffering and humility continue in the work of being God's servants. The early Christian hymn recorded in the book of Philippians provides a New Testament expression of this conviction by emphasizing self-emptying love as the way that Christians are called to imitate Christ (2:5-7). What Paul proclaims here is something seen in Jesus and something Jesus knew from God's revelation to Israel in Isaiah 53. God prefers to partner with servants. Jesus is the best example of this servant identity and is *the* Suffering Servant, even as Israel came to share in God's redemptive work through its experience of exile.

God's Ongoing Presence in the Covenant Community

Alongside the nature of God's saving work and how God partners to accomplish it in the world, the Servant Song in Isaiah 53 testifies to God's ongoing presence in the covenant community, especially in times of loss and suffering. The prophet's message to the exiles clearly indicates that God has not abandoned them and continues to work among them.

Moreover, Israel was God's partner, and it took on the task as a people to embody the presence of God for the nations (Isa. 49:6). Israel took on the role of a humbled and suffering servant in the midst of the Babylonian exile so that it could demonstrate that the power of God remains active and has not been defeated by the forces of empire. As Israel embodied servanthood in suffering, and as Jesus did the same, modern readers can see a model for living as God's people today. We can be agents of God's loving work as part of the covenant community by taking on actions that mirror those embodied by Israel and Jesus.

Caution is in order, however. Isaiah 53 should not create a desire to claim some badge or prize for suffering. Additionally, the call to experience and embody God's presence through suffering and service must not be used to justify oppression or to keep people in oppression by telling them that they need to suffer. Even so, service is a demand set upon God's people. But as with Israel in exile, it is often something God's people do collectively. For example, although Martin Luther King Jr. was rightly honored with the 1964 Nobel Peace Prize, he joined with many thousands of people who partnered in the civil rights movement and who suffered in servanthood for the abiding care of other humans, thus extending the witness and work of God in the world. The abiding presence of God is made known when God's people are willing to embrace collectively the call to become persons who have "no form or majesty" or "nothing in . . . appearance" to be desired (Isa. 53:2, NRSV). Rather, they follow the model of the ancient people of Israel and the person of Jesus to take on "suffering" and become "acquainted with infirmity" (v. 3, NRSV). When Christians work to give health care to the poor or provide justice for the underserved, they partner with the afflicted and stricken (v. 4). When Christians lift the lowly and bring care to the disadvantaged, they embody God's loving presence in the midst of suffering.

Reflection

Isaiah 52:13–53:12 expresses the larger Old Testament themes of God's saving work, especially for the oppressed, suffering, and marginalized, and God's ongoing presence in the covenant community and the world. Consider some of these practices and questions concerning the calling upon God's people today:

1. What experiences in life might compare to Israel's exile and the sense of having lost God's presence or being excluded from God's work in the world? How does Isaiah 53 reaffirm God's presence and a role for God's people in the midst of suffering?

2. Identify some concrete ways that you see the church in your community actively serving others. What additional opportunities for service can you consider?

3. Share some examples of where you have seen God enter situations of loss and suffering and use them for good. In what ways could Isaiah 53 be an encouragement for people in difficult situations?

10
EZEKIEL 36:26
Thomas J. King

I will give to you a new heart, and a new spirit I will put within you,
and I will remove the heart of stone from your flesh,
and I will give to you a heart of flesh.
—Ezekiel 36:26

Ezekiel 36:26 in the Old Testament

Exile and Sense of Abandonment

The book of Ezekiel brings us to the exilic period of Old Testament history. Like its more familiar predecessor, the exodus event (associated with Israel's slavery in Egypt), the exile was a time of confinement in a foreign country. The exilic period was not characterized by enslavement and forced labor (as in Egypt), but it did represent an experience of overwhelming loss and banishment from the homeland. The Babylonians had overthrown Judah, destroyed Jerusalem, and exiled the majority of Judeans by forcing them to live in Babylon. Most devastating was the destruction of the temple, which represented the place of the presence of God among the people in Judah. It is difficult enough to lose one's home and be expelled from one's country, but the thought of one's God being overthrown and driven out, as evoked by the razing of the temple, would have been more than many Judeans could endure. The event likely dissolved all hope for many who survived the attack and were carried away into exile.

The people of Judah had certainly been warned over the previous two centuries that something like this was coming if the nation did not change its ways. The prophets had preached against idolatry and injustice and had warned the people about the consequences of forsaking their covenant relationship with the Lord. Early in the exilic period, Ezekiel had a vision depicting the unimaginable for the children of Israel. He saw the presence (glory) of the Lord abandoning the temple, moving first out to the entrance (Ezek. 9:3; 10:4), then to the east gate of the outer courtyard (10:18-19), and finally away over the Mount of Olives (11:22-25).[1] The departure of the Lord was the result of defilement stemming from the sins of the people. Through Ezekiel's preaching, the Lord identified bloodshed and idolatry among the sins that led to Israel's dispersion (36:18-19).

Jacob Milgrom, while discussing the function of the purification offering, explains how the sins and impurities of Israel polluted the sanctuary and temple even from a distance (Lev. 15:31; 20:3; Num. 19:13, 20) and threatened God's abandonment of the temple.[2] This created an urgency to cleanse the temple from sin and impurity regularly in order to avoid the unthinkable.

> Finally, why the urgency to purge the sanctuary? The answer lies in this postulate: the God of Israel will not abide in a polluted sanctuary. The merciful God will tolerate a modicum of pollution. But there is a point of no return. If the pollution continues to accumulate, the end is inexorable: "Then the cherubs raised their wings" (Ezek 11:22). The divine chariot flies heavenward, and the sanctuary is left to its doom. The book of Lamentations echoes this priestly

---

1. Stephen L. Cook, "Ezekiel," in *The New Oxford Annotated Bible*, 5th ed., ed. Michael D. Coogan (Oxford, UK: Oxford University Press, 2018), 1188.

2. Jacob Milgrom, *Leviticus 1–16*, The Anchor Bible 3 (New York: Doubleday, 1991), 256-58.

theology: "The Lord has abandoned his altar, rejected his Sanctuary. He has handed over to the foe the walls of its citadels" (Lam 2:7).[3] Ezekiel portrayed this very catastrophe through his vision of the abominations in the temple (Ezek. 8:6-18) and the departure of the glory of the Lord.

Ezekiel, who is identified as a priest (1:3), clearly reflects priestly theology with a significant concern for the temple and purity. The early chapters of the book of Ezekiel express judgment against Israel's rebellious acts, which defiled the holiness of God's temple and forced God to withdraw (Ezek. 8–11). In conjunction with God's withdrawal from the temple, the people of Israel were scattered (specifically in this context Judah was exiled to Babylon). The dispersion among the nations brought about the defilement of God's holy name as the nations recognized that the Lord's people had been expelled from God's land (36:20). These two events (abandonment of the temple and exile for the people) represent the major expressions of judgment for Israel's sin and apostasy. However, as is true for most of the Hebrew prophets, judgment was not the last word for Ezekiel. Judgment was intended to drive Israel to repentance as a means of facilitating the ultimate goal of reconciliation. Consequently, it is not surprising to see Ezekiel turn to oracles of hope and restoration, such as the one expressed in Ezekiel 36:22-32.

Judgment and Restoration

In response to the aftermath of destruction, loss, and exile, Ezekiel expressed hope and renewal through the oracles of restoration that characterize chapters 33–48 of the book. In general, Ezekiel 1–24 consists of judgment oracles, and chapters 33–48 primarily communicate oracles of restoration. In between, chapters 25–32 contain "oracles against the nations," commonly found in many of the Prophetic Books of the Hebrew

---

3. Ibid., 258.

Bible.[4] The themes of judgment and restoration are tied to the absence and presence of God, as illustrated by God's departure from the temple in Ezekiel 8–11 and God's return to a new temple in Ezekiel 40–48. Most striking, however, is the depiction of God's presence in Ezekiel 1–3 in Babylon among the exiles.

Ezekiel's priestly theology would normally associate God's presence almost exclusively with the temple in Jerusalem. The depiction of God's departure due to the impurity of the temple and God's return to a new purified temple aligns with a priestly view of God's presence in relation to holiness. However, the appearance of God's presence in Babylon among the exiles who have been expelled due to sin and impurity is unexpected. While the vision of Ezekiel 1–3 provides the context for Ezekiel's commission, the picture of God's presence among the exiles expresses a profound message of grace. God came to Israel in the midst of their impurity in an unclean land in direct contrast to the foundational understanding that God cannot abide impurity. It suggests that God's love for Israel is greater than any aversion to sin and impurity. This is the same God who in Christ dined with sinners, touched lepers, and befriended outcasts (e.g., a Samaritan woman, a tax collector, etc.).

God came to Israel in the midst of their impurity in an
unclean land in direct contrast to the foundational
understanding that God cannot abide impurity.

Ezekiel's vision also highlights God's sovereignty as a divine being who is not limited as a regional god but exercises the freedom of the God

4. J. Gordon McConville, *A Guide to the Prophets*, vol. 4 of *Exploring the Old Testament* (Downers Grove, IL: InterVarsity Press, 2002), 17.

of the universe. The imagery in Ezekiel 1 even creates "a visual representation of [YHWH's] sovereignty over the entire cosmos."[5] This message
of love and power laid a foundation early in the book of Ezekiel for hope
grounded in God's promise of restoration for the exiles.

Cleansing and Restoration

God's Holiness among the Nations: Ezekiel 36:22-23, 31-32

The words of the Lord that begin the opening and closing verses of
our passage (vv. 22, 32) serve to envelop the section with a proclamation
of judgment: "*not* for your sake am I about to act" (emphasis added). Verse
32 continues with the clarification that Israel should "be ashamed" and
"dishonored" (or "humiliated") by the ways in which they have behaved.
The previous verse (v. 31) indicates that the people of Israel will remember
their "evil ways" and their "bad deeds" and loathe themselves due to their
"iniquities" and "abominations." The verse is clearly packed with synonyms
for wrongdoing that seem to immerse Israel in its disgrace. In response,
God acted to bring cleansing and renewal to Israel.

Normally, prophetic texts move from judgment to a call for repentance before describing God's promises of restoration. Milgrom reminds
readers that priestly theology requires forms of repentance (remorse and
confession) in order for intentional, rebellious sins (as those described in
Ezek. 36) even to be eligible for atonement.[6] For Ezekiel, repentance
takes the form of shame and contrition as expressed in verses 31-32. Such
penitence makes Israel eligible to worship in the new sanctuary, before the
presence of the Lord. "Thus, Ezekiel is informed: 'When they [the people]

---

5. Brad E. Kelle, *Ezekiel*, New Beacon Bible Commentary (Kansas City: Beacon Hill
Press of Kansas City, 2013), 73.

6. Milgrom, *Leviticus 1-16*, 301-2.

are ashamed of all they have done, make known to them the plan of the sanctuary' (Ezek 43:11a)."[7]

A devastating result of Israel's sin, as described above, is the pollution of the sanctuary (the place of God's presence). This pollution is generally described as "defilement" by means of the Hebrew term *tame'*. An egregious example of defiling God's sanctuary is identified as sacrificing one's child to the pagan god Molech (Lev. 20:3). Such an act is echoed in the combination of bloodshed and idolatry condemned in Ezekiel 36:18. The Leviticus passage describes the result of such sin as defiling (*tame'*) God's sanctuary and profaning God's holy name (20:3b). These are the very concerns addressed by Ezekiel. The pollution of God's sanctuary was discussed above in relation to the broader context of Ezekiel. The profaning of God's holy name is the subject to which we now turn.

The remainder of the opening statements for this passage (Ezek. 36:22-23) identifies the motive for God's action as the sanctification of God's holy name. Verses 22 and 23 together contain three instances of the root *qadash* ("holy," "to consecrate"; once as a noun and twice as a verb) contrasted with three instances of the verb *chalal* (to profane). These terms reflect the divergent realms whose distinction is the responsibility of the priesthood (Lev. 10:10-11). An important task of the priests of Israel is "to enlarge the realms of the sacred and the pure by reducing the areas of the common and the impure."[8] Ezekiel 36:22-32 speaks to this very task. The opening and closing verses of the passage highlight how Israel has profaned the name of the Lord in contrast to God's declaration to consecrate (make holy) God's name. This envelops the central portion of the passage (vv. 24-30), which describes God's work of cleansing and purifying Israel.

The sanctification of God's name is not magnified for the sake of Israel alone. It is explicitly concerned with reaching the nations. The defilement brought about by Israel's iniquities is explicitly described as

---

7. Jacob Milgrom and Daniel I. Block, *Ezekiel's Hope: A Commentary on Ezekiel 38–48* (Eugene, OR: Cascade Books, 2012), 44.

8. Milgrom, *Leviticus 1-16*, 616.

profaning God's holy name "among the nations" (vv. 22-23). In response, God will consecrate God's holy name so that "the nations shall know that I am the LORD" when the Lord manifests God's holiness "before their [the nations'] eyes" (v. 23). This concern for the nations expresses a foundational Old Testament theme. It is expressed as early as God's call to Abraham in Genesis 12. The final statement in God's speech commanding Abraham to "go forth from your country" expresses God's intention that through Abraham "all the families of the earth will be blessed" (v. 3). This is an early indication of God's purpose for the election of Israel, which is to reach the nations. The same concern is implicit in God's covenant with Israel as expressed at Mount Sinai. While describing Israel's election as those who are God's own possession "among all the peoples" (Exod. 19:5), God calls Israel to be "a kingdom of priests and a holy nation" (v. 6). If the entire kingdom was to be made up of priests, then the intended congregation must have been *the nations*. This very calling is what Ezekiel proclaims Israel has failed to accomplish. In contrast, Israel has profaned God's name "among the nations" (Ezek. 36:22-23). The nations recognized God as a failure because they saw that Israel had been exiled (v. 20). This puts in jeopardy God's plan to reach the nations. Therefore, Ezekiel announced God's intention to act to restore the holiness of God's name. It is noteworthy that God's means of sanctifying God's name includes proving God holy "*through you* [Israel] before their [the nations'] eyes" (v. 23; emphasis added). This statement evokes Israel's role as a kingdom of priests through whom the nations should come to know God and God's holy name.

The structure of the passage as described earlier emphasizes God's work of restoring Israel. The enveloping arrangement of the text points to the middle portion of our passage as that which conveys the heart of the message. Once again, judgment (vv. 22-23, 31-32) is not the last word, but it surrounds and thereby highlights the central proclamation of the passage, which is a grace-filled message of cleansing and renewal (vv. 24-30).

Cleansing and Divine Fellowship: Ezekiel 36:24-25

The center of this passage (vv. 24-30) expresses God's declaration to cleanse and renew Israel. God's initial promise was to return Israel to its own land (v. 24). This act would serve to reverse the dispersion that prompted the nations to consider God as having failed with God's own people (v. 20). The second promise was to transform the people of Israel. God's promise to transform Israel is detailed through a series of divine activities aimed at restoration (vv. 25-30).

God pledges to cleanse the people of Israel by "*tossing* clean water" upon them (v. 25; emphasis added). Priestly literature displays a strong tendency toward formulaic terminology that often carries distinctive meanings. Ezekiel's use of the Hebrew term *zaraq* ("to toss," "to throw," "to dash") is uncharacteristic here compared to the normal priestly application of the term. While some consider the use of *zaraq* and *nazah* (to sprinkle) as synonymous in the priestly material, an examination of their occurrences in the Old Testament demonstrates very specific and distinct applications, with few exceptions.

Common use of the term *nazah* reflects collateral dispersion, such as the accidental spatter of blood on a priest's garments (Lev. 6:27 [Hebr. v. 20]; see also Isa. 63:3 with regard to lifeblood spattered on garments), and a person's blood splattered against the wall (2 Kings 9:33; see also the uncertain text at Isa. 52:15 meaning either "sprinkle" or "startle"). All other appearances of the verb *nazah* in the Old Testament function ritually in the following contexts: (1) the ordination *consecration* for Aaron and his sons by means of "sprinkling" blood and oil on them (Exod. 29:21; Lev. 8:30 [see also v. 11, consecration of the altar]); (2) the *dedication* of the Levites upon whom the unique water of purification was "sprinkled" (Num. 8:7); (3) *cleansing* from leprosy by means of "sprinkling" a mixture of blood, cedar wood, crimson yarn, and hyssop (on persons [Lev. 14:7] or on homes [v. 51]; oil was also "sprinkled" before the Lord as part of the cleansing rite for leprosy [vv. 16, 27]); and (4) the rite of the *purification offering* in which blood was "sprinkled" in relation to the altar (5:9; 16:19), the curtain of the sanctuary (4:6, 17), the mercy seat (16:14-15), and the tent of meeting (Num. 19:4; the red heifer is designated a purification offering at v. 9). The term *nazah* appears in only one other passage (vv. 18-19, 21), which will be addressed below. At this point, the ritual use of the term can be summarized as functioning especially in relation to the purification offering, as well as priestly consecration, cleansing from leprosy, and the purification of the Levites. These rites clearly reflect the themes of *cleansing* and *consecration*. These themes are certainly in view in Ezekiel 36:25 as evidenced by the triple use of the Hebrew root *taher* for "clean" and "cleanse." So it is surprising that Ezekiel does not use the term *nazah* (to sprinkle) in this verse.

Common use of the term *zaraq* expresses the idea of "throwing" something through the air: Moses "threw" soot in the air (Exod. 9:8, 10); Josiah "tossed" dust onto graves (2 Chron. 34:4); Job's friends "threw" dust in the air onto their heads (Job 2:12); the "tossing" of cumin when planting (Isa. 28:25); and burning coals "tossed" down over the city of Jerusalem (Ezek. 10:2). A final text expresses how gray hairs are "tossed" or "scattered" on one's head (Hos. 7:9). In relation to ritual passages *zaraq* is used almost exclusively in relation to *burnt offerings* and *well-being offerings* (in distinction from *nazah*, which is used in relation to the purification offering as described above). In relation to burnt offerings and well-being offerings, *zaraq* is used to describe how the blood of the offerings was "tossed" or "dashed" *against the altar* (Exod. 24:6; Lev. 1:5, 11; 3:2, 8, 13; 7:14; 9:12, 18; 17:6; 2 Kings 16:13, 15; 2 Chron. 29:22; 30:16; Ezek. 43:18). To this list must be added the two rams of the ordination offering; the first of which is explicitly identified as a burnt offering (Lev. 8:18-19; see also Exod. 29:16), and the second follows the rite of the first by also having its blood "dashed" against the altar (Exod. 29:20; Lev. 8:24). The term *zaraq* is also used for "dashing" the blood of the *guilt offering* against the altar (Lev. 7:2). Reference is made to the burnt offering in the same verse, and the guilt offering carries a similar function to that of the burnt offering: "The guilt offering is not as concerned with cleansing the altar, as it is with expressing invocation and devotion (reflecting the functions of the burnt offering; [see] 1:3) in relation to seeking restitution (the primary concern of the guilt offering; Budd 1996, 117)."[9] Also, *zaraq* is used to "dash" the blood of firstborn offerings against the altar (Num. 18:17). Milgrom states that these firstborn sacrifices were to be treated as well-being offerings.[10] Finally, we see *zaraq* used once in relation to "dashing" the blood of the Passover lamb (2 Chron. 35:11). The Passover lamb relates to the well-being offering as one whose meat is shared with the common person (see v. 13; alternatively "the blood that they received" and "dashed" in v. 11 could refer to the burnt offerings mentioned in the following v. 12). The ritual use of *zaraq* can be summarized as functioning in relation especially to the burnt offering and the well-being offering, reflecting the purposes of invocation, devotion, and fellowship with the Lord. These appear to be themes upon which Ezekiel draws in order to supplement the focus on cleansing in Ezekiel 36:25.

Most pertinent to the use of *zaraq* in our Ezekiel passage (36:25) is the application of blood, oil, or water *to persons*. The application of such symbolic fluids to persons only occurs with the verb *nazah* ("sprinkling"; to consecrate or purify Aaron and sons, leprous persons, and Levites as described above). There are three exceptions to this, in which the verb *zaraq* (not *nazah*) is found in relation to fluids being applied *to persons* (otherwise, *zaraq* in ritual contexts is found only in relation to applications *against the altar*). The unique use of *zaraq* in ritual applications to persons suggests an intentional deviation from the norm in which *nazah* is used in relation to persons and sancta (such as the tent of meeting, the altar, the mercy seat, and before the curtain). The three exceptional uses of *zaraq* in application to persons include the rite of the red heifer in Numbers 19 and in Exodus 24:8, along with our text of Ezekiel 36:25.

---

9. Thomas J. King, *Leviticus*, New Beacon Bible Commentary (Kansas City: Beacon Hill Press of Kansas City, 2013), 89, citing Philip J. Budd, *Leviticus*, New Century Bible Commentary (Grand Rapids: Eerdmans, 1996), 117.

10. Jacob Milgrom, *Numbers*, JPS Torah Commentary (Philadelphia: Jewish Publication Society, 1990), 153.

The rite of the red heifer is aimed at purifying the person who is defiled by touching a corpse. The red heifer is explicitly identified as a purification offering (Num. 19:9, 17), so we expect the use of *nazah* in this passage (see above), as indeed it occurs in verses 18-19, 21. The appearance of *zaraq* in this rite, and its application to persons, stands out as exceptional (vv. 13, 20). It suggests the addition of the themes of devotion and divine fellowship to the dominant concern for purification that characterizes the cleansing of the corpse—contaminated person. In his discussion of the use of *zaraq* in Numbers 19:13, Levine proposes that Ezekiel was referring to rites such as that of the red heifer when he spoke of God's purification of Israel in Ezekiel 36:25.[11] While purification is the foundational concern, the unusual use of *zaraq* where *nazah* is expected highlights the addition of devotion and divine fellowship as themes that these texts seek to convey.

The second exceptional use of *zaraq* for persons, Exodus 24:8, is part of a covenant ceremony between God and the people of Israel. The ceremony involves burnt offerings and well-being offerings (v. 5); thus we expect the use of *zaraq* and the "dashing" of blood "against the altar" as indeed occurs in verse 6. The unexpected occurs, however, when Moses takes half the blood of the offerings and "dashes" (*zaraq*) it upon *the people* (v. 8). This covenant-making ceremony calls for the people's commitment to God, and the dashing of blood serves as "a means of consecrating Israel as [YHWH's] holy people."[12] Sarna reminds readers that blood, which represents life and belongs exclusively to God, must be returned to God by being dashed on the altar. The very unique dashing of blood *on the people* in this covenant ceremony creates a mysterious bond between the covenant parties. God symbolically shares the blood, and thereby "the life of the recipient is thought to take on a new dimension and to be elevated

11. Baruch A. Levine, *Numbers 1–20*, The Anchor Bible 4A (New York: Doubleday, 1993), 466.

12. John I. Durham, *Exodus*, Word Biblical Commentary 3 (Waco, TX: Word Books, 1987), 344; see also 343.

to a higher level of intimate relationship with the Deity."[13] Ezekiel 36:25 participates in this unique use of *zaraq* depicting the "dashing" of symbolic fluid (in this case, water) *on people*. It suggests that Ezekiel evokes the idea of intimate relationship with God. This elevated dimension of *new life* for Israel (water, like blood, is often associated with life) is dramatically portrayed in the very next chapter of Ezekiel through the vision of dry bones that are vividly restored to *new life* (37:1-14).

The foundational concern expressed in Ezekiel 36:25 is cleansing-purification. This is evident by the threefold use of the term *taher* (clean): "I will dash upon you *clean* water and you will be *clean* from all your impurities, and from all your idols I will *cleanse* you" (emphasis added). Both impurity and idolatry are highlighted as the sources of Israel's uncleanness. God promises to graciously cleanse Israel. In addition, the prophet draws upon another significant theme in the Old Testament: God's desire for intimate relationship with people. The unique use of *zaraq*, associated with the themes of devotion and divine fellowship, reflects God's desire to raise Israel to a new level of life and covenant relationship.

New Heart and New Spirit: Ezekiel 36:26-27

In addition to cleansing the people of Israel, God promised to place a new heart and new spirit within them (v. 26). In fact, it was to be God's own Spirit that would be placed in the people of Israel (v. 27). The old heart of stone, which is depicted as hardened and stubbornly fixated on sin, was to be replaced with a heart of flesh evoking that which is malleable and free to reason. In Hebrew anthropology the heart is the center of rational function, including knowledge and the will.[14] This new heart reflects what we would consider to be a new mind. This transformation

---

13. Nahum M. Sarna, *Exodus*, JPS Torah Commentary (Philadelphia: Jewish Publication Society, 1991), 152.

14. Hans Walter Wolff, *Anthropology of the Old Testament*, trans. Margaret Kohl (Philadelphia: Fortress Press, 1974), 46-55.

prefigures the apostle Paul's exhortation for believers to "be transformed by the renewing of your mind" (Rom. 12:2, NIV).

God enables and inspires the people to obedience;
God does not constrain their ability to choose.

God's implanting of a new heart and spirit within Israel portrays a profound transformation. Given the long history of Israel's (and humanity's) sin and rebellion (from its origins in Eden through the flood, judges, and kings and up to Israel's exile in Babylon), God turned to radical surgery. The result of this dramatic act raises provocative questions about Israel's new condition. God proclaims to Israel, "I will make it such that you will walk in my statutes and you will carefully observe my judgments" (Ezek. 36:27). Milgrom argues that this reflects "Ezekiel's utopian vision of Israel's transcendent 'sainthood.'"[15] The new heart and new spirit from God signify that Israel will no longer sin. Israel will be incapable of disobedience. As described in verse 27, the people will be programmed to faithfully obey God's commands and will not choose evil again.[16] This view creates significant tension with the foundational commitment to human free will, enabling genuine relationships, which is expressed throughout the Old Testament. Kelle points out the ambiguity of the Hebrew wording in verse 27 and suggests that the NIV translation may be more helpful here: "And I will put my Spirit in you and *move you* to follow my decrees and be careful to keep my laws" (emphasis added). The implication is that God enables and inspires the people to obedience; God does not constrain their ability to choose. This is more consistent with Ezekiel's

---

15. Milgrom and Block, *Ezekiel's Hope*, 263.

16. Ibid., 264; see also 43-44.

statements later in the book exhorting Israel to obey laws aimed at maintaining the holiness of the new temple.[17]

Renewed Land: Ezekiel 36:28-30

The theme of new things (new heart and new spirit) in the context of exile is shared by the prophets Isaiah and Jeremiah. Isaiah speaks of God doing a "new thing" in relation to the promise of returning the exiles through a renewed wilderness (Isa. 43:19-21). Jeremiah describes a "new covenant" that God will initiate with Israel and Judah (Jer. 31:31). Both Jeremiah and Ezekiel bind these *new* movements to the *old* foundational covenant grounded in the law of God. Even though Jeremiah writes "It will not be like the covenant that I made with their ancestors" (v. 32*a*, NRSV), the new covenant is nevertheless identified with the same old *law* that will now be written upon the hearts of the people (v. 33*a-b*). Furthermore, Jeremiah uses the old covenant formula, "I will be their God, and they shall be my people" (v. 33*c*, NRSV; see Exod. 6:7; Lev. 26:12), to identify the new covenant. This same formula is repeated in Ezekiel 36:28, and the old *law* is what Israel will be inspired to obey, as expressed in verse 27. This links God's work of restoration for the exiles to a renewal of the old covenant relationship.

Verses 28-30 express God's promise to return the exiles to their land and to cause the land to produce abundantly. The theme of fruitful land for Israel originates with God's promise to Abraham and his descendants, initially expressed with God's call for Abraham to go "to the land that I will show you" (Gen. 12:1, NRSV) and God's promise to give that land to Abraham's descendants (v. 7; 17:8). The promise was passed down through the generations of Isaac and Jacob and ultimately to the children of Jacob-Israel. The abundance and good produce of the promised land is often characterized by the formulaic phrase "a land flowing with milk and honey" (Exod. 3:8; Lev. 20:24; Num. 13:27; Deut. 26:9). Earlier in the book, when rehearsing Israel's history of rebellion and idolatry, Ezekiel recalled

---

17. Kelle, *Ezekiel*, 298-99; see also 60-61.

the land flowing with milk and honey (Ezek. 20:6, 15). That is the land to which Israel was to be restored.

God promised twice in a row that the land would be fruitful and would not yield to famine (36:29-30). This is expressed through the multiplying of grain and the multiplying of the fruit of the tree and the produce of the field. In an agrarian society this was a promise of abundant provision. Juxtaposed with the promise of abundance is the twice-repeated promise that Israel will not be disgraced by, or bear the reproach of, famine. Famine represented the absence of God's provision and thereby the alienation of God's presence due to Israel's apostasy. The concluding phrase of verse 30, "among the nations," recalls the indictment of verses 22-23 accusing Israel of profaning God's name among the nations. Famine drives the people of Israel to other nations in order to find food and produce, thereby exposing Israel's alienation from the God who provided for them.[18] In the context of Israel's cleansed and renewed life in relationship with God, famine will no longer pose such a threat.

Reflection

Read Ezekiel 36:22-32 once again and identify words, phrases, and statements that reflect the following Old Testament themes: holiness of God, sin and defilement, cleansing, restoration and renewal, covenant relationship, confession and repentance, and concern for all nations.

---

18. Moshe Greenberg, *Ezekiel 21-37*, The Anchor Bible 22A (New York: Doubleday, 1997), 731.

11
JOEL 2:28
Stephanie Smith Matthews

> *I will pour out my spirit upon all flesh.*
> —Joel 2:28*a*

Joel 2:28 in the Old Testament

Joel was one of the Latter Prophets, likely writing in the fifth century BCE. This was after some of the Jewish people had returned from exile. The Assyrian and Babylonian Empires had deported and resettled the ruling classes far from their ancestral homelands in an attempt to weaken cultural ties and lessen opportunities for rebellion against the empires. The northern tribes of Israel experienced this at the hands of Assyria in 722 BCE (2 Kings 17). After unsuccessfully aligning themselves with the Egyptian Empire, officials in Jerusalem, the capital of Judah, were first deported by the Babylonian Empire in 597 BCE (2 Kings 24). Following a rebellion against Babylonian rule, Jerusalem and its temple were taken, and a second deportation was enacted in 586 BCE (2 Kings 25).

In 539 BCE, the Babylonian Empire had been taken over by King Cyrus of Persia. Cyrus's approach to subduing local people groups was different from that of his predecessors. Cyrus allowed resettled peoples to return to their homelands. Many among the Jewish people returned to Jerusalem, where they rebuilt the temple (Ezra 1) and the city walls (Neh. 1). They remained under Persian rule, paying Persian taxes, but living and worshipping with a certain level of autonomy—so long as they did not form political alliances against their rulers.

This is the setting in which the prophet Joel brought forth a message from God for Jerusalem (Zion).

Joel 1-2

As we open the pages of the book of Joel, we see that a locust invasion has utterly destroyed the food sources for people and for animals (1:16-18).[1] Throughout Joel 2, the imagery is ominous, giving us the sense of being crowded in. The locust horde, described as a devouring army from the north (vv. 3-5, 20), has turned a land "like the garden of Eden" into a "desolate wasteland" (v. 3b).

The description of locusts coming as an army from the north is an apt one. A horde of locusts could come swift and terrifying, with swarms converging and darkening the sky (v. 10). This comparison also draws from Jerusalem's history of warfare. Allusions to a devouring northern army call to mind the Assyrian and Babylonian armies that entered the region through routes north of the kingdoms of Israel and Judah. Joel describes the locusts that could indiscriminately "rush into the city, run over the [city] wall, go up into houses, and go through windows like a thief" (v. 9). Elsewhere in the Old Testament we find a description of a Babylonian army that entered the city of Jerusalem and "killed youths by the sword in the house of their sanctuary, without pity for young man or woman, elder or aged" (2 Chron. 36:17). And just as devouring locusts destroyed every food source in sight, so, too, could ancient warfare practices involve starvation. Before their city was finally breached, the sixth-century BCE inhabitants of Jerusalem—trapped for over a year inside the walls meant to defend them—experienced a "famine [that] was so strong in the city there was no food for the people of the land" (2 Kings 25:3; Jer. 52:6).

---

1. Locust swarms continue to impact food security in portions of Africa and across southern Asia.

In this way, the imagery at the beginning of the book of Joel allows for more than one entry point. Its poetic language and symbolism may invoke a locust swarm, a threatening army, or, for readers living in different situations, other forces that threaten life. Just as Joel pulled from his biblical traditions, using their symbolic power to describe the devastation of his day, so may we. We, too, may identify where "people are in anguish" (Joel 2:6), where "food [is] cut off before our eyes [and] joy and gladness from the house of our God" (1:16).

At the end of this description, Joel describes the entrance of the Lord. At first, God seems to be on the side of the terror and destruction: "The LORD gives his voice before his army, for very big is his camp; many are those who enact his word. Indeed, the day of the LORD is great and very feared. Who can contain it?" (2:11). When we experience great anguish and suffering, we may ask, "Is this God at work?" (see 1 Kings 17:20). Others may even tell us this is so. Joel and his audience, like those of the cultures around them, believed their God was ultimately in control of the weather and wild animals, indeed the entire ecosystem. These people would turn to God, asking for an intervention to save them—to return their land and community into a place of flourishing.

A Response to Imminent Disaster

In the wake of such a desolate opening to the book, Joel 2:12 marks a clear transition. Perhaps more arresting in its original Hebrew, the opening phrase, "'And moreover, now,' declares the LORD," slows us down from the thundering charge of the northern army (and our anxious response). What follows is a call to turn to God. In other places in the Old Testament, the call to turn to God is clearly to turn away from sin. In those cases, the word is translated "return" or "repent." In other cases, it is rendered simply "turn," as in most translations of God's activity in verse 14. Perhaps the ambiguity allows us to read the verse either way, depending on our circumstance. We may find ourselves in need of repentance and turning back to God. Or it may be that our need to turn to God arises from situations other than our own sin. Whatever the situation, the call from God in Joel 2:12 is to "turn to me with all your heart."

Despite the NRSV's inclusion of the word "punishing" in verse 13, the Lord (speaking through Joel) does not mention from what the people are to turn. By reading both before and after these verses, we can, however, gain a sense of what God is now calling the people to do as they turn to God. The content of the first two chapters has painted a vision of terror and distress. Indeed, the word of the Lord through the prophet Joel in chapter 1 was to "hear" (v. 2), "wake up" (v. 5), "lament" (v. 8), "wail" (vv. 11, 13), and "cry out" (v. 14) to the Lord concerning their calamity. Joel 2:12-13 asks the people to fast, weep, mourn, and to "rend [their] hearts." In other words, they were to lament and cry out about their suffering to God. In chapter 1, Joel had already called on the people to lament their condition. Here, the call is made to direct such lamentation to God as an act of prayer.[2]

Despite what remains unclear, what questions
we may have, even how others may have misrepresented
God to us, we can trust in the character of God
as loving and trustworthy.

This section of Joel offers an opportunity for self-examination. Do we value lament and cries of suffering as acts of prayer? Do we join others

---

2. Examples of this kind of prayerful response to calamity may be found in Lamentations, within the book of Psalms, and throughout portions of the Prophetic Books in the Old Testament. Jesus even quoted the opening line of a psalm of lament (Ps. 22) as he was dying on the cross (Matt. 27:46; Mark 15:34). For more on lament in the Old Testament, see the chapter in this volume by Christina Bohn, "Psalm 13:1."

in their laments in solidarity as communal worship? Or do we flout such biblical examples and discourage the honest acknowledgment of our pain and suffering? The lesson from Joel is that we do not have to stop crying out in order to be faithful to God. All that is asked of us at this point is to orient ourselves toward God as we do so.

The description of God that follows is one of encouragement to a suffering people. In light of such questions as "Is this disaster from God?" we are reminded of the character of God as affirmed throughout the Old Testament: "[God] is gracious and merciful, slow to anger, and abounding in steadfast love" (2:13, NRSV). This is a quotation from Exodus 34:6. It evokes covenant language: it establishes the relationship between God and God's people, as well as God's character as loyal to the people and always honoring the terms of their relationship. God is someone we can trust to turn to with everything in our lives. Despite what remains unclear, what questions we may have, even how others may have misrepresented God to us, we can trust in the character of God as loving and trustworthy.

In his description of God's character, Joel leaves off the rest of the quotation from Exodus and concludes with a line that has given translators some trouble. Biblical Hebrew is a language in which one word may have several meanings, which we determine based on the context of the passage it is in. Sometimes, however, the surrounding context is not enough for the translator to be absolutely certain about which meaning is best. In fact, sometimes a biblical poet seems to be making a play on words (such as repeating the same Hebrew word to refer to all of humanity, a particular man, and the name of Adam in Gen. 1–5) or intentionally selecting a word with an ambiguous meaning, recognizing that the way we choose to translate it reflects our own theological beliefs. For example, in Job 42:6 we are told that Job "repents," "is sorry," "grieves," or "comforts himself." Each of these is a faithful translation of the same Hebrew word. And each could lead to quite a different sermon about Job! In other contexts, the word can mean to "have pity on" or to be "moved to compassion" for others.

As it happens, the same Hebrew word appears in Joel's statement about God at the end of 2:13. In addition to being "gracious and merciful, slow to anger, and abounding in steadfast love," God grieves, is sorry for, and is moved to compassion by distress. Whether God will always intervene to put an end to the harm is less clear to Joel: "Who knows? [God] may turn and be moved to compassion and may leave behind a blessing, an offering and libation for the LORD, your God" (v. 14). Even the prophet Joel does not know for certain what is to come. Being assured of God's character did not make clear everything the people could expect about their future. And yet their reaffirmation of the nature of their loving God led them to hope that just maybe that compassion would result in a restoration of food and drink. That God might somehow provide the very grain and wine they wished they could offer up to the Lord (see 1:13).

Although in the Old Testament we are not always assured of what will happen in life, even for those who faithfully follow God, we are assured again and again of the character of God: "gracious and merciful, slow to anger, and abounding in steadfast love"—a God moved with compassion when those in this world suffer distress. We can turn to our philosophers, theologians, and religious historians to help us make sense of the existence of suffering in a world created by a loving God. Sometimes the answer is clear enough: God allows us free will, and we can choose to harm others, and they suffer as a result of our callousness and sin. But other types of suffering defy such explanation, and we find ourselves in the "Who knows?" portion of Scripture. Far from a flippant dismissal, such a posture is one of hope—based on the character of God and on a humility about our own ability to divine all truth in this life. The "Who knows?" also calls forth the question, "Can we be part of the solution?" God often works through creation, partnering with us, to embody God's compassion in the world.

Communal Response: Lament and Celebration

At the very center of the book of Joel, the people respond to the call to turn to God. In 2:15-17, all the people of Jerusalem assemble, from the eldest in the congregation to the babies still nursing at their mothers' breasts. The priests and ministers lead the way in weeping and crying out to God. In this instance, Joel reports that God does respond with compassion for both the land and the people suffering along with it. God's answer is a promise to send the grain, wine, and oil they lacked—so much so as to fill them up, to satiate their hunger and thirst (v. 19). Lest God's initial response has been missed, God repeats the vision of restoration in a rallying cry to plants, animals, and people alike (vv. 20-27). Earlier in the chapter, God welcomed cries of lamentation; now God encourages creation to be glad and rejoice (vv. 21, 26) at the Lord's restoration of life. Note what happened to change lament to rejoicing. Life was restored! Suffering was ministered to. Circumstances changed! *That* was something to celebrate.

As we step back from the specific circumstances that gave rise to the prophecy in the book of Joel, we may observe the themes expressed therein. The vivid descriptions of human suffering and terror, as well as expressions of both anguish and jubilation, represent the full expression of human experience to which the Old Testament bears witness. Furthermore, we see that this expression of human experience and emotion is recognized in the community and directed to God. Indeed, the character of our God is the very thing that calls us to be honest about our present circumstances and, at the same time, to look beyond them in hopeful imagination.

Joel 2:28

With bellies full and celebration on our lips, we turn to our focus verse (v. 28), joined inseparably to the verse that immediately follows (v. 29). As we saw with Joel 2:12, the opening phrase of 2:28 marks a clear shift in the flow of Joel's prophetic utterance. Translated rather woodenly, it would read, "And it will happen after this [that] . . ." (v. 28a). This rather wordy introduction once again interrupts the steady flow of God's promises in the verses prior: "I will repay" (v. 25), "You will eat" (v. 26), and "You will know" (v. 27). Each of these springs forth without prior introduction. Our promise in verses 28-29 could have begun similarly: "I will pour out." Instead, we are offered a pause.

This change in language, as well as the rather abrupt shift in imagery to come in verse 30, leaves even biblical scholars uncertain of the relation of verses 28-29 to the surrounding passages. An illustration of this is that the Christian canons (following the ancient Greek translation known as the Septuagint) place these verses at the end of chapter 2, whereas the Jewish canon (following the tradition of Hebrew manuscripts) marks them as the beginning of chapter 3. In the New Testament book of Acts, Peter quotes Joel 2:28-29 and those that follow them in his response to the powerful pouring out of the Holy Spirit at Pentecost (Acts 2:16-21).

Many of us may have been introduced to these verses in Joel through their quotation in Acts but are less familiar with how this prophecy fits in to the book of Joel. Here is an outline of the book of Joel, organized around the themes each passage discusses:

    I. (1:1–2:11) Telling the story of the destruction of the land

    II. (2:12-17) Return to/turn to and call on the Lord

    III. (2:18-27) Fulfillment of safety as needs are met

    IV. (2:28-29) God's Spirit poured out on all people

    V. (2:30-32) Troubling signs and salvation for those who call on the Lord

    VI. (3:1-21) Restoration of Judah and Jerusalem, with judgment on the nations for the nature of the harm they caused to others

As we have seen, the book of Joel begins with a story of desolation and destruction caused by a devouring northern army (of locusts). The people are called to turn and cry out to God, who is characterized as one who is loyal and caring. In the third movement of this prophetic book, the people know safety yet again as their basic needs are met. In this they are experiencing *shalom*, the peace and flourishing of the community. At the end of the prophecy, all references to actual locusts have fallen away and are replaced by images of atrocities committed by humans against one another. God is affirmed as the defender who will judge those who have shed innocent blood (3:16, 19).

Perhaps images of a northern army have awakened the collective memory of the calamities brought by all manner of warfare. Thus the book begins and ends with troubling scenes. Yet at its core are dual messages of salvation and, nestled between them, our promise of the pouring out of God's Spirit:

> After this
> I will pour out my spirit upon all flesh:
>> your sons and your daughters will prophesy;
> your elders will dream dreams;
>> your youths will see visions.
> Indeed, upon your male and female slaves
>> in those days I will pour out my spirit. (Joel 2:28-29)

The promise of the Holy Spirit would come to be associated with many powerful and empowering acts. Here, however, we see a specific promise: the ability to prophesy—that is, receiving and proclaiming God's word to the community. Perhaps in response to our tendency to place limits on the ways we expect God to act—through whom we assume God can speak—God adds a little specificity to that phrase "all flesh" (v. 28). Who comes to your mind when you hear the words "preacher," "pastor," or "proclaimer of God's Word"? Now, joining with the earliest hearers of Joel's prophecy, allow God to expand your theological vision. Your sons *and your daughters* will proclaim God's Word. The elders of the community *as well as* its youths will cast glorious visions of God's kingdom on earth. The power of God's Spirit will be on display among those most abused by societal structures, beginning with the enslaved. Lest any improper assumptions be made that God cannot speak through someone, God proclaims through the prophet Joel an expansive vision of the work of the Spirit of God through "all flesh."

Old Testament Themes in Joel 2:28-29

This promise of God and its place in the book of Joel lead us to several themes that help acquaint us with the Old Testament. The promise of the Spirit in Joel 2:28 follows an intense focus on human experiences of both suffering and joy. God's presence is affirmed within a covenant community—and all that entails. What's more, God chooses to work in powerful ways through individuals who might appear to some as unexpected choices.

Human Life and Experience of the World

Perhaps one of our most pressing questions as we attend worship services or listen to sermons is, "How does this apply to us now?" Or to state it another way, "What difference does this Word make in my life right now?" Answering such questions is a matter of deep prayer and discernment on the part of believing communities and for those ministering among them. But perhaps we might pause for a moment and marvel at the very fact that our life experiences do matter to God. One gift of the Old Testament is its strong witness to the meeting place between humans and God. Whether we suffer or celebrate or experience the two comingled, the Bible calls us to turn with those experiences to God.

Joel 1–2 depicts the power of lament and of sharing the story of our suffering with one another and with God. Joel's prophecy describes the devouring of land by locusts and recalls the horrors of warfare and economic oppression that seek to obliterate the very image of God present in all flesh. The prophet calls people to turn and bring their suffering to God. This is very different from a call to ignore, fix, or make sense of suffering *before* turning to God.

It is not only in times of sorrow that we turn to God but also in times of rejoicing. Upon experiencing their salvation, the children of Zion are to "rejoice and be joyful with the LORD [their] God" because God has been the source of their salvation (2:23). Taken collectively, Joel 1–2 taps into the Old Testament theme of bringing the fullness of our human experience to God. Crucially, the promise of the Spirit in Joel 2:28-29 comes after great attention has been paid to specific human experiences of suffering, salvation, and joy. Perhaps as we grant holy attention to the experiences of ourselves and others, we, too, will encounter a pouring out of the Spirit of God.

God's Presence in the Covenant Community

Within my culture, religion, salvation, and sanctification are often discussed as individual experiences. Yet the book of Joel tells of communal suffering, salvation, rejoicing, and receipt of the Spirit. The inclusivity of Joel 2:28-29 also reaches out to individuals who have been overlooked in our religious communities. It affirms that God's Spirit can work powerfully through any one of us—and tells the rest of our community to expect it! In this way, these verses are meant to shape our communities.

All of this communal language is a part of the Old Testament theme of God's relationship with a covenant community. This covenantal relationship was shaped by the people's commitment to God's *torah* ("instruction" or "law"). Jewish and Christian interpreters liken the pouring out of the Spirit of God to the softening of hearts (Ezek. 36:26) and the ability to collectively follow God's *torah* (Jer. 31:33). We may summarize *torah* as Jesus did: to love God and love neighbor. The Old Testament vision of a community shaped by such love is one marked by *shalom*—peace, human flourishing, and life.

God did not simply deliver a set of guidelines and leave the people alone to follow them. The Old Testament, as we see in the book of Joel, is concerned with God's presence within the covenant community. In Joel, the promise of God's Spirit comes just one verse after God's affirmation that "you will know that I am in your midst" (2:27). What is it that will help them to know? They will see the restoration of their food sources. They will once again know flourishing.

We might consider this a lesson to us. How do others know if God is in the midst of our communities? If we follow the example of Joel, it is by attending to the fullness of our human experience, sharing that experience with one another and with God, and seeking our collective flourishing. Then people shall know that God is in our midst, and through such practices we may be prepared to bear witness to the Spirit of God in our communities.

An Expansive Vision of God's Presence

Returning to the specifics of Joel 2:28-29, we may celebrate God's egalitarian pouring out of the Spirit. Persons and religious movements have found in Joel 2:28-29 and its interpretation in Acts 2 support for an expanding vision of God's community on earth that goes beyond our usual categories and distinctions. For holiness traditions, it is the community's recognition of the Holy Spirit at work in an individual that is supposed to confirm his or her calling as a minister of the gospel. Our own categories may differ from those listed in Joel, or they may be the same. Practice living in expectation of God's Spirit showing up. If we never expect to encounter God's Spirit in another, how will we recognize it when it comes? Let us not miss out on the healing, restorative joy of the Spirit of God showing up among us to transform us into communities of flourishing, of *shalom*.

Reflection

Joel 2:28-29 reflects the Old Testament themes of God's preferences and partners—working through persons and communities that are often unheralded—as well as God's ongoing presence in the covenant community and the world, past, present, and future. As a response to this passage and its themes, commit to the practices of Joel 1–2:

1. Who among you suffers? Take time to share and lament. Turn to God in prayer with the fullness of these experiences.

2. Seek the restoration—the fullness of salvation—of those in need among you. How can you partner with God to change the circumstances of suffering to those of rejoicing?

3. Who among you has cause to rejoice? Take time to share and celebrate. Invite God into your times of celebration.

4. Affirm the Spirit of God at work among you. Have serious discussions about your limitations as a community. Do you tend to affirm certain

persons and not others? Ask God to reveal the fullness of God's vision for our communities—through the power of the Holy Spirit!

12
MICAH 6:8
Beth M. Stovell

He has shown you, O mortal, what is good.
And what does the LORD require of you?
To act justly and to love mercy
and to walk humbly with your God.
—Micah 6:8, NIV

Micah 6:8 in the Old Testament

Micah 6:1-8 is located in the part of the Old Testament known as the Book of the Twelve Prophets or the Minor Prophets. As the sixth book of the Twelve, it functions as a transition between the first six books and the second six books. The first six books of the Twelve (Hosea, Joel, Amos, Obadiah, Jonah, and Micah) share the general setting of the eighth century BCE prior to the Assyrian destruction of Israel (cf. 2 Kings 14–20; 2 Chron. 26–32), while the second half of the Twelve shifts predominantly to the period after the Babylonian destruction of Jerusalem and the exile in the early sixth century BCE (cf. 2 Kings 24–25; 2 Chron. 36:1-21). Some of these reflect the specific setting of Israel's return from exile in the late sixth century BCE (cf. 2 Chron. 36:22-23; Ezra 1).

In the overall story of the Old Testament, when we arrive at Micah 6, the people of Israel have become a nation through their forefather Abraham, they have received the law through Moses, and they have even come to live in the land that God promised Abraham and Sarah so many generations before. But Micah 6 also comes at a time of crisis. The once united monarchy of Israel under King David and his son Solomon has divided into two kingdoms: the Northern Kingdom of Israel and the Southern Kingdom of Judah. The two kingdoms struggle with one another and with the surrounding nations. We learn in Micah 1:1 that "Micah of Moresheth" received a "vision . . . concerning Samaria and Jerusalem" (the capital cities of the Northern and Southern Kingdoms respectively) from the Lord "during the reigns of Jotham, Ahaz and Hezekiah, kings of Judah" (NIV). The prophet Jeremiah later cites the prophecy of Micah of Moresheth in defense of Jeremiah's own prophecy (Jer. 26:18). This defense saves Jeremiah from the death penalty. Jeremiah describes how Micah prophesied during King Hezekiah's reign. Hezekiah reigned in the Southern Kingdom of Judah in the eighth century BCE. Micah's prophecies overlap with the prophecies of Isaiah, Hosea, and Amos, coming slightly after these three prophets.

As with Isaiah, Hosea, and Amos, Micah describes the way that the people of Israel have turned away from God and toward different kinds of injustice and oppression. The sins of Israel are related not only to its relationships with the surrounding nations but also to its oppression of its own people. Micah describes this injustice in gruesome ways, comparing it to skinning and eating the people alive (Mic. 3:1-4). While the people of Israel put on a show of worshipping God, similar to what we see in Isaiah 58, their hearts have turned away from God and away from love of their neighbor.

God's Case against Israel: Micah 6:1-7

The prophet's message in Micah 6:1-8 begins with God putting Israel on trial (v. 1). Because God is the great creator of all the world, the witnesses called for this case are not people but creation itself: God calls the mountains and hills to listen to the case being presented against Israel (v. 2). It helps to remember that God's relationship with Israel is a covenant agreement. Covenant agreements in the ancient world were signed documents, with both parties agreeing to fulfill certain conditions or stand in violation of the covenant. Often these agreements were between great kings and lesser kings. God puts Israel on trial because it has violated its end of the covenant.

Verse 3 moves from God's call to the mountains and hills to an opening question, as God asks Israel, "My people, what have I done to you?" (NIV). God follows up this first question with a second one: "How have I burdened you?" (NIV). God expects an answer, but Israel does not give one. It is likely there is no answer from the people because they know that God has not burdened them. What God has done for the people was the opposite of a burden. God has shown them from the beginning divine love and grace.

Verse 4 picks up on one of the major themes we find elsewhere in the Old Testament: God is the one who has saved Israel in the past. God delivered the people from their slavery in Egypt, bringing them out and redeeming them (Exod. 13–14). Additionally, God gave them leaders to guide them through the wilderness in the figures of Moses, Aaron, and Miriam. Thus the question of Micah 6:3 hangs in the air: What has God done to this people? Instead of being a burden, God saved them. But their actions show that they have forgotten this act of grace.

Verse 5 alludes to two more stories that the people should "remember" so that they will know God's righteous acts on their behalf. The first is the story of Balak, the king of Moab, and his plots with Balaam, son of Beor. The names "Balak" and "Balaam" point to a story in Numbers 22–24. Balak, the king of Moab, hires Balaam, a non-Israelite prophet, to curse the Israelites so that they will perish in the wilderness on the way to the promised land. Instead, Balaam experiences one of the funniest scenes in the Bible: God uses Balaam's own donkey to talk to him. The donkey becomes a prophet for the Lord! In the end, Balaam blesses the Israelites instead of cursing them. While there is debate about whether Balaam is actually a heroic figure in Numbers, Micah 6 cites Balaam as an example of

God using a prophet to speak against a king who plotted to destroy Israel.[1] This story demonstrates God's repeated care in unexpected ways.

The second story that God asks the people to remember in verse 5 is their journey from Shittim to Gilgal. While it is possible that the phrase "Shittim to Gilgal" simply refers to Israel's trip across the Jordan River into the promised land and God's care during that time, the prophet might use this phrase ironically.[2] In Hosea, Micah's contemporary, Baal-peor (a place associated with Shittim) and Gilgal are commonly associated with Israel's wickedness and idol worship (Hos. 9:10-15). Seen in this way, Israel must remember two things: God's righteous acts toward it and Israel's contrasting rebellion against God at the same time.

Verse 6 seems like a strange transition from the voice of the Lord speaking to Israel to what sounds like the voice of the prophet Micah musing about what the Lord wants from him and imagining how an audience member might respond to the Lord's words. All this talk of the Lord's righteous acts in verses 4-5 inspires Micah to wonder what righteous acts he must do, what sacrifices at the altar God wants. What could Micah do to repair the damage that Israel has done by acting with oppression and violence in its own community? Verse 6 builds on the sacrificial system described in Leviticus. Micah begins reasonably enough and suggests sacrificing burnt offerings to God. Part of the life and character of the covenant community has been responding to God through such sacrifices, making itself declared "holy" by doing the sacrifices the right way based on the laws set out in Leviticus (for example, see the laws concerning the burnt offering in Lev. 1).

But Micah wants to make a point, so he gradually intensifies the sacrifices he might give to the Lord. First, the burnt offerings are not just any burnt offerings but calves that are one year old. The mention of the age

---

1. Dennis T. Olson, *Numbers*, Interpretation (Louisville, KY: Westminster John Knox Press, 2012), 140-42.

2. Carolyn Sharp, *Irony and Meaning in the Hebrew Bible* (Bloomington, IN: Indiana University Press, 2009), 148-51.

of the calves might point back to Leviticus 9:3, where the ordination of Aaron, the first high priest, includes specifically a one-year-old calf. Thus Micah's first proposed offerings are not ordinary; they are like the offering presented when the first high priest took on his role.

Micah 6:7 abruptly pushes this overly abundant sacrifice to extraordinary levels. Rather than proposing a single burnt offering of a ram, as we see Abraham offer in place of his son Isaac in Genesis 22, Micah asks whether he should offer thousands of rams. He teams these thousands of rams with ten thousand rivers of olive oil. The increasing abundance is significant. This is not ten thousand oil offerings, but so many oil offerings that they become ten thousand flowing *rivers* of oil offerings.

But Micah isn't done with raising his potential offerings past the point of reason or expectation. He ends his list of possible overabundant sacrifices with the question of whether he must offer his own firstborn. He offers his firstborn because his transgressions (and the transgressions of Israel) are so great. Micah suggests that the only way to absolve the greatness of his sin might be to sacrifice the very fruit that comes from himself, to slaughter a part of himself represented by his firstborn son and to offer it to God through his son. This final suggested offering draws the reader back to Abraham's willingness to sacrifice Isaac, but it also reminds us that God does not want this kind of sacrifice. Behind Micah's final offer is the question, Would even this be enough?

The Surprising Climax: Micah 6:8

Just as Micah reaches his crescendo of overabundant and overly painful offerings, verse 8 acts as a climax that stops readers in their tracks. Micah's questions are answered because God has already shown every human being (mortal) what is desired. God has shown what is good and what is required of every person. Verse 8 provides the climax that causes the reader to listen carefully. If all of the potential sacrifices of Micah were not enough, what will be enough? The answer appears at first overly simple. God desires three actions: (1) "act justly," (2) "love mercy," and (3) "walk humbly with your God" (NIV).

Preliminarily, notice that the phrase "what is good" in verse 8 echoes back to the start of the Old Testament when God created the world. God saw all that had been created and said that "it was good" and "it was very good" (Gen. 1:10, 12, 18, 21, 25, 31, NIV). Micah frames his question of what God wants within the bigger picture of God as the one who created the world in goodness and desires goodness back from his people. Additionally, the phrase "what . . . the LORD require[s]" (Mic. 6:8, NIV) connects back to Micah's list of sacrifices in verses 6-7. Leviticus frequently speaks of doing what the Lord requires or keeping the Lord's requirements (e.g., Lev. 8:35; 18:30). Micah 6:6-7 already questioned whether the sacrificial system is the simple answer to the question, "What does the LORD require of you?" (v. 8, NIV). Now in verse 8, Micah introduces another way to answer this question in the form of three actions.

"To Act Justly"

The first of the three-part answer to the questions, "What is good?" and "What does the LORD require?" is "To act justly." This idea of just action needs to be understood in the broader context of the Old Testament. First, Leviticus and Deuteronomy not only list the Lord's sacrificial requirements but also provide an emerging picture of justice that includes poverty laws to protect the most vulnerable in Israel's society: the orphans, the widows, the poor, and the foreigners living in the community's midst (Lev. 19; 25–26; Deut. 10:17-19; 14:28-29). In these passages, God reminds the people of their experiences as the oppressed and as foreigners in Egypt to soften their hearts toward the ones hurting in their community.[3] This shows that God's justice includes a special care for the oppressed and the marginalized.

---

3. For more on what this might mean for ministry with immigrants today, see Beth M. Stovell, "Moving from 'Them' to 'Us': A Biblical Theology for Diaspora Ministry," in *Beyond Hospitality: Migration, Multiculturalism, and the Church*, eds. Charles Cook, Lauren Goldbeck, and LoraJoy Tira-Dimangondayao (Toronto, ON: Tyndale Academic Press, 2020), 28-38.

God's justice includes a special care for
the oppressed and the marginalized.

Setting these laws in their ancient context is helpful. Law codes created by ancient Near Eastern kings in the regions neighboring Israel describe these kings as caring for the oppressed. We see this in the famous Code of Hammurabi, which claims that the Babylonian gods gave King Hammurabi (ca. 1810–ca. 1750 BCE) his kingship so that he might be a "king of justice," with laws created "in order that the strong might not oppress the weak, that justice might be dealt the orphan (and) the widow . . . to give justice to the oppressed."[4] Even so, these law codes themselves do not include any actual laws that protect orphans, widows, or the oppressed. Instead, this language served as propaganda to make the people happy with their king while actually experiencing continued oppression. In contrast, not only does the Old Testament provide specific laws in Leviticus and Deuteronomy to protect these very people, but also, since Israel repeatedly violated these laws, Israel's prophets spent much of their time reminding the people that these laws were still active and important to God. The prophets of Micah's time were particularly vocal in this regard, as we see in Isaiah 58 and Amos 5. These prophets were calling Israel back to laws that God already put in place. Instead of following these laws, the people and their leaders violated them in the worst way possible: by oppressing the most vulnerable among them.

Micah demonstrates these acts of oppression by Israel earlier in the book. His picture of this injustice in chapter 3 is particularly gruesome.

---

4. See Norbert Lohfink, "Poverty in the Laws of the Ancient Near East and of the Bible," *Theological Studies* 52 (1991): 34-50.

Micah 3:2-3 compares the Israelites' injustice to cannibalism, killing their own people in order to consume them. Micah 3 shows that oppressing the vulnerable not only violates God's laws to care for them but also is disgusting violence, in which rulers and leaders, the ones in power, consume their people for their own gain.

Micah 6:8 provides a sharp contrast. The prophet declares that the answer to the questions, "What is good?" and "What does the Lord require?" is, first, "To act justly." Instead of injustice and oppression, Micah reminds Israel and all humanity that God has already shown them how to discern good from evil (to use the language of Mic. 3) and how to do what God requires. The first step is to act justly. This form of justice is not as simple as individual sacrifices but involves overhauling the systems of violence and injustice in their midst (see Mic. 3). Thus to act justly is to restructure the systems that hurt the vulnerable, the widow, the orphan, the poor, and the foreigner.

"To Love Mercy"

The second part of the answer in verse 8 to the questions, "What is good?" and "What does the Lord require of you?" is, "To love mercy." The theme of loving mercy extends throughout the Old Testament. Loving mercy builds on acting justly as mercy and justice work hand in hand. The word "mercy" comes from the Hebrew word *ḥesed* (steadfast love), which is used to describe God's own character in Exodus 34:6. This character trait abounds in God. God is known for steadfast love toward Israel. Many of Micah's fellow prophets in the Book of the Twelve quote the language of Exodus 34:6-7 to talk about God's loving mercy and Israel's response, as does Micah in other parts of the book. Joel 2:13 describes how the people can lament over their sin, return to God, and receive love and mercy. Micah quotes Exodus 34:6-7 more directly in Micah 7:18-19, where he asks who is like God in having this character. God "pardons sin and forgives the transgression of the remnant of his inheritance." God "[does] not stay angry forever but delight[s] to show mercy" (v. 18, NIV). God will again have compassion on God's people and "tread our sins underfoot and hurl all our iniquities into the depths of the sea" (v. 19, NIV). Likewise, Jonah 3:9 and 4:2 also quote Exodus 34:6, but in this case, Jonah is angered by this divine character trait. Jonah does not want God to be gracious to the Ninevites or show them any mercy. Yet God will do this anyway because of God's character. Jonah talks about how he is angry with God because God is "slow to anger and abounding in [steadfast] love" (4:2, NIV). In other words, Jonah is angry that God loves mercy.

In contrast to Jonah, Israel is asked to love this aspect of who God is—to embrace God's slowness to anger and tendency toward love, mercy, and compassion. Micah 6:8 reminds the people that not only are they to love this aspect of who God is, but they are supposed to live this characteristic out in their own lives as well.

To turn toward mercy with love is to embrace God's call to
a righteousness that is embodied as a right relationship
with the world around us.

Loving mercy is more than a nice sentiment, however. Placed alongside the verbs "act" and "walk" in verse 8, this kind of love assumes action. Love involves a turning toward another in mercy rather than a turning away. To turn toward mercy with love is to embrace God's call to a righteousness that is embodied as a right relationship with the world around us. Just as "act justly" calls us to overhaul systems of injustice, so does "love mercy" call us to love with the shocking, unwavering, sometimes upsetting mercy received by those who turn toward God. As we see in Jonah's example, this may mean forgiving those we deem unforgivable and yielding to God's mercy, even when it angers us to do so.

"To Walk Humbly with Your God"

If acting justly leads to loving mercy, then both of these lead to the third part of the answer to the questions, "What is good?" and "What does the LORD require of you?": "To walk humbly with your God." While acting with injustice made the people of Israel numb to God's goodness, acting justly offered a way to restructure their lives toward God's original intention of peace and wholeness. While Jonah's hate of God's mercy blinded him to God's love, loving mercy offered Israel a way to learn from God's own character of mercy and compassion. This third and final action of walking humbly with God provides Israel a path back to God's intended journey for them.

Walking humbly with God is rooted in the broader metaphor of "walking" found in Old Testament Wisdom Literature, such as Proverbs and part of the Psalms. In the Old Testament, the verb "walk" is often used metaphorically to compare the idea of physical walking with the broad concept of journeying with God. In these biblical passages, this verb "walk" is often accompanied by the language of "ways," "paths," and "feet." While "ways" and "paths" describe directions and pathways a person might choose to follow, "feet" points to the part of the body a person would use to walk along that path. This is the grammatical device known as "synecdoche," where a smaller part represents a bigger part. "Ways" and "paths" represent the entire journey, and "feet" represent the entire person who takes that journey. Sometimes these are all summed up by simply using the verb "walk" to encompass the entire picture of this journey.[5]

Proverbs sets up a contrast between those who walk with God in wisdom, following God's laws, continuing on God's pathways, and those who reject this path and walk in foolishness, walking with the wicked, on paths that lead to destruction. Proverbs begins by describing two paths that someone could take: the path of sinful people (1:10-19) or the path

---

5. See Phil Botha, "Following the 'Tracks of Righteousness' in Psalm 23," *Old Testament Essays* 28, no. 2 (January 2015): 283-300.

of "Lady Wisdom," who calls out in the streets and asks people to listen to her and follow her ways (vv. 20-33; 2:1-9). This path language—wisdom-righteousness or foolishness-wickedness—continues throughout Proverbs (e.g., 2:9, 15, 18; 4:11, 26; 5:6, 21).

The book of Psalms also describes the two pathways that someone could *walk*: the way of the wicked or the way of righteousness. Psalm 1 begins by saying, "Blessed is the one who does not *walk* in step with the wicked," the one "whose delight is in the law of the Lord" (vv. 1-2, NIV; emphasis added). The Psalms repeatedly talk about what comes from *walking* with the Lord. This includes "truth" (15:2), "comfort" (23:4), deliverance and the "light of life" (56:13), "favor and honor" (84:11), dwelling with God (101:6), "freedom" (119:45), and salvation (138:7) (all NIV). Micah 6:8 builds on this long wisdom tradition. God wants Israel to walk in God's paths. These paths are ones that follow God's laws, that seek God's presence, and that lead toward life rather than toward destruction.

Micah 6:8 adds an important facet to *how* the people of Israel should walk with God. They should walk "humbly." This theme of humility before God also appears elsewhere in the Old Testament. Deuteronomy 8 speaks repeatedly about God's goal in humbling the Israelites as they journeyed in the wilderness after God freed them from Egypt. This humbling was intended to be a test to show how much the hearts of the people were actually turned toward and dependent on God (vv. 2-3, 16). In Joel 2:12, God calls Israel to return with all their hearts "with fasting and weeping and mourning" (NIV), signs of humility. Notably, this verse is followed by verses 13-14, which quotes Exodus 34:6 and the proclamation of God's mercy (see above). Second Chronicles 7:14 also provides a helpful picture of what this humility might look like: "If my people, who are called by my name, will *humble themselves* and pray and seek my face and turn from their wicked ways, then I will hear from heaven, and I will forgive their sin and will heal their land" (NIV; emphasis added). Like Micah 6:8, this Chronicles passage speaks of the people "humbling" themselves, but it also uses the language of "ways." As noted above, part of the broader metaphor of "walking" includes the language of "ways" alongside "paths" and "feet."

From Micah's use of the broader traditions of walking and humility, we can see that in Micah 6:8, the action of "walk[ing] humbly with your God" implies a lifelong journey. This journey involves acknowledging the destructive paths we have taken in the past, as well as the choice to return to God and to God's ways, which are the pathways of wisdom. In doing so, we do what is good and what the Lord requires, and we chart a pathway toward the "land of the living" (Ps. 116:9, NIV).

Micah 6:1-8 as a Wake-Up Call for God's People

On the one hand, Micah 6:8 does not tell the Israelites anything new. Yet, on the other hand, it functions as a wake-up call, an important reminder of what the Israelites already know about who God is and who God has called them to be. God's character was always one of justice and steadfast love (mercy) that called for a lifelong walk that was humble before God. The calls to the Israelites to be holy as the Lord was holy always intended them to follow God by acting justly, by showing mercy through steadfast love like God's love, and by walking before God with an obedience that showed a humble reverence for God. Micah 6:8 places the reminder of "what is good" and "what . . . the LORD require[s]" at a moment in Israel's life when the people have forgotten their big story and their big God. As they journeyed deeper and deeper into oppressive actions and unjust ways to benefit themselves, as they lost their mercy toward others and their humility before God, they slowly forgot who this God was that their ancestors had served. They grew to expect only goodness from God and no rebuke, thinking their regular sacrifices were enough. Micah 6:1-8 is intended to wake them up to the reality that their sacrifices were never about a show of righteousness, all pretty on the outside, but were intended to represent a heart of righteousness on the inside that cared for the poor and the vulnerable and acted in line with God's holiness.

Just as God presented the divine court case by repeatedly calling Israel to "remember" in verses 4-5, so does the prophet's proclamation in verse 8 call the people to remember their first love (as Hos. 2:7 puts it) and to remember God's love as their creator, savior, and model for what justice and love look like.

Reflection

Micah 6:1-8 engages the larger Old Testament themes of the character of the covenant community's life with God and others, especially through the practice of justice and righteousness. Take some time to reflect on what it might look like today for you to act justly, love mercy, and walk humbly with God.

1. Thinking about justice as well-being for the marginalized and vulnerable, what systems (political, economic, and religious) in our world today result in inequity and injustice for the marginalized and vulnerable in our communities? How could you be part of changing these systems right now?

2. How could we "love mercy" today? Are there people with whom you wish God would remain angry and from whom you wish God would withhold mercy? How can you overcome those feelings? What acts of loving-kindness could you do today in your neighborhood?

3. What keeps you from "walk[ing] humbly with your God" today? Do you need God to remove your pride, your self-sufficiency, or your dependence on other things? What is one step you could take today to "walk humbly with your God"?

BIBLIOGRAPHY

Berman, Samuel A., ed. and trans. *Midrash Tanḥuma-Yelammedenu: An English Translation of Genesis and Exodus from the Printed Version of Tanḥuma-Yelammedenu with an Introduction, Notes, and Indexes*. Hoboken, NJ: KTAV Publishing House, 1996. https://www.sefaria.org/Midrash_Tanchuma %2C_Vayera.22?lang=bi.

Botha, Phil. "Following the 'Tracks of Righteousness' of Psalm 23." *Old Testament Essays* 28, no. 2 (January 2015): 283-300.

Brueggemann, Walter. *Reverberations of Faith: A Theological Handbook of Old Testament Themes*. Louisville, KY: Westminster John Knox Press, 2002.

Bullón, Dorothy. "The Missionary Movement of the Nineteenth Century." *Didache: Faithful Teaching* 14, no. 1 (Summer 2014). https://didache.nazarene .org/index.php/volume-14-1/1030-didache-v14n1-07b-19th-cent-missions -bullonen/file.

Cairns, Ian. *Word and Presence: A Commentary on the Book of Deuteronomy*. International Theological Commentary. Grand Rapids: Eerdmans, 1992.

Clements, Ronald E. "The Book of Deuteronomy." Pages 853-1052 in vol. 1 of *The New Interpreter's Bible*. Nashville: Abingdon, 2015.

Clifford, Richard J. "Introduction to Wisdom Literature." Pages 1-16 in vol. 5 of *The New Interpreter's Bible*. Nashville: Abingdon Press, 1997.

Crenshaw, James L. *Old Testament Wisdom: An Introduction*. Atlanta: John Knox Press, 1981.

Ferguson, Niall, ed. *Virtual History: Alternatives and Counterfactuals*. New York: Basic Books, 1997.

Fretheim, Terence E. *Exodus*. Interpretation. Louisville, KY: Westminster John Knox Press, 2010.

————. *God and World in the Old Testament: A Relational Theology of Creation*. Nashville: Abingdon Press, 2005.

Gafney, Wilda. *Womanist Midrash: A Reintroduction to the Women of the Torah and the Throne*. Louisville, KY: Westminster John Knox Press, 2017.

Goldingay, John. *Genesis*. Baker Commentary on the Old Testament Pentateuch. Grand Rapids: Baker Academic, 2020.

Janzen, J. Gerald. "On the Most Important Word in the Shema." *Vetus Testamentum* 37, no. 3 (1987): 280-300.

Kelle, Brad E. *Ezekiel*. New Beacon Bible Commentary. Kansas City: Beacon Hill Press of Kansas City, 2013.

Kelle, Brad E., and Stephanie Smith Matthews, eds. *Encountering the God of Love: Portraits from the Old Testament*. Kansas City: Foundry, 2021.

King, Thomas J. *Leviticus*. New Beacon Bible Commentary. Kansas City: Beacon Hill Press of Kansas City, 2013.

Levine, Baruch A. *Numbers 1–20*. The Anchor Bible 4A. New York: Doubleday, 1993.

Lohfink, Norbert. "Poverty in the Laws of the Ancient Near East and of the Bible." *Theological Studies* 52 (1991): 34-50.

McConville, J. Gordon. *A Guide to the Prophets*. Vol. 4 of *Exploring the Old Testament*. Downers Grove, IL: InterVarsity Press, 2002.

Meyers, Carol. *Exodus*. New Cambridge Bible Commentary. Cambridge, UK: Cambridge University Press, 2005.

Milgrom, Jacob. *Leviticus: A Book of Ritual and Ethics*. A Continental Commentary. Minneapolis: Fortress Press, 2004.

———. *Leviticus 1-16*. The Anchor Bible 3. New York: Doubleday, 1991.

———. *Numbers*. JPS Torah Commentary. Philadelphia: Jewish Publication Society, 1990.

Milgrom, Jacob, and Daniel I. Block. *Ezekiel's Hope: A Commentary on Ezekiel 38–48*. Eugene, OR: Cascade Books, 2012.

Morales, L. Michael. *Who Shall Ascend the Mountain of the Lord? A Biblical Theology of the Book of Leviticus*. New Studies in Biblical Theology 37. Downers Grove, IL: InterVarsity Press, 2015.

Murphy, Roland E. *The Tree of Life: An Exploration of Biblical Wisdom Literature*. Grand Rapids: Eerdmans, 1990.

Nelson, Richard D. *Deuteronomy: A Commentary*. The Old Testament Library. Philadelphia: Westminster John Knox Press, 2004.

Olson, Dennis T. *Numbers*. Interpretation. Louisville, KY: Westminster John Knox Press, 2012.

Pokrifka, H. Junia. *Exodus*. New Beacon Bible Commentary. Kansas City: Beacon Hill Press of Kansas City, 2018.

Sarna, Nahum M. *Exodus*. JPS Torah Commentary. Philadelphia: Jewish Publication Society, 1991.

Sharp, Carolyn. *Irony and Meaning in the Hebrew Bible*. Bloomington, IN: Indiana University Press, 2009.

Stovell, Beth M. "Moving from 'Them' to 'Us': A Biblical Theology for Diaspora Ministry." Pages 28-38 in *Beyond Hospitality: Migration, Multiculturalism, and the Church*. Edited by Charles Cook, Lauren Goldbeck, and LoraJoy Tira-Dimangondayao. Toronto, ON: Tyndale Academic Press, 2020.

Tolkien, J. R. R. *The Hobbit, or There and Back Again*. New York: Random House, 1982.

United States Catholic Conference. *Catechism of the Catholic Church: Complete and Updated*. Washington, DC: USCCB, 1995.

Wenham, Gordon J. *The Book of Leviticus*. The New International Commentary on the Old Testament. Grand Rapids: Eerdmans, 1979.

Whelchel, Michael Eugene. "The Relationship of Psychological Type to the Missionary Calling and Cross-Cultural Adjustment of Southern Baptist Missionaries." DMiss diss., Asbury Theological Seminary, 1996.

Wolff, Hans Walter. *Anthropology of the Old Testament*. Translated by Margaret Kohl. Philadelphia: Fortress Press, 1974.

Yancey, Philip. *Reaching for the Invisible God*. Reprint, Manila: OMF Literature, 2000.

ABOUT THE AUTHORS

Editors

Brad E. Kelle is professor of Old Testament and Hebrew at Point Loma Nazarene University. He received his PhD in Old Testament from Emory University and holds additional degrees in biblical studies and theology from Trevecca Nazarene University and Candler School of Theology at Emory University. An ordained elder in the Church of the Nazarene, he is the author of numerous scholarly books and articles, including *The Bible and Moral Injury: Reading Scripture alongside War's Unseen Wounds* and *Telling the Old Testament Story: God's Mission and God's People*. He is also the author of *Ezekiel* in the New Beacon Bible Commentary series and coeditor with Stephanie Smith Matthews of *Encountering the God of Love: Portraits from the Old Testament*. The latter two books are available from The Foundry Publishing.

Stephanie Smith Matthews is assistant professor of Old Testament and Hebrew at Point Loma Nazarene University. She received her PhD in Hebrew Bible and ancient Israel from Vanderbilt University, where she was a Lilly Fellow in Theology and Practice. She holds additional degrees in biblical studies and theology from Olivet Nazarene University and the University of Notre Dame. She is coeditor with Brad E. Kelle of *Encountering the God of Love: Portraits from the Old Testament* and contributor to *Following Jesus: Prophet, Priest, King*. Both books are available from The Foundry Publishing.

Contributors

Christina Bohn is assistant professor of Old Testament at MidAmerica Nazarene University. She is the coauthor of *Genesis 12–50* in the New Beacon Bible Commentary series.

Derek Davis is associate dean of academic programs and enrollment and instructor of biblical languages at Nazarene Theological Seminary, where he has taught Greek and Hebrew for the last ten years.

Timothy M. Green is dean of the Millard Reed School of Theology and Christian Ministry and professor of Old Testament Literature and Theology at Trevecca Nazarene University. An ordained elder in the Church of the Nazarene, he is the author of various publications, including *The God Plot: Living with Holy Imagination* and *Hosea–Micah* in the New Beacon Bible Commentary series.

Thomas J. King is professor of Old Testament at Nazarene Bible College. He is an ordained elder in the Church of the Nazarene and author of *Leviticus* in the New Beacon Bible Commentary series.

Jennifer M. Matheny is associate professor of Old Testament and director of the Wynkoop Center for Women in Leadership at Nazarene Theological Seminary. She is the author of *Joshua* in the Illustrated Hebrew-English Old Testament series and *Judges 19–21 and Ruth: Canon as a Voice of Answerability*.

Kevin J. Mellish is professor of biblical studies at Olivet Nazarene University. In addition to several published articles and book chapters, he is the author of *1 and 2 Samuel* in the New Beacon Bible Commentary series.

Marty Alan Michelson retired as professor of Old Testament from Southern Nazarene University. He continues to teach for various universities, Nazarene Bible College, and Nazarene Theological Seminary. He has served churches internationally and in America. He is a licensed mental health professional in multiple states.

Mitchel Modine is professor of Old Testament and director of the MDiv program at Asia-Pacific Nazarene Theological Seminary. He is an ordained elder in the Church of the Nazarene and the author of *Numbers: A Pastoral and Contextual Commentary*.

Stephen P. Riley is director of academic assessment at the University of Denver. He previously served as associate professor of Old Testament and Hebrew at Northwest Nazarene University. He is an ordained elder in the Church of the Nazarene and coeditor of *God Still Calls: Discerning God's Direction for Service*.

Beth M. Stovell is professor of Old Testament and chair of General Theological Studies at Ambrose University in Calgary, Alberta. Having worked for over twenty years in ministry, Beth currently oversees theological consultation with her husband, Jon Stovell, on the national team for Vineyard Canada. She has authored numerous books and articles, including *Biblical Hermeneutics: Five Views* (with Stanley Porter) and *Making Sense of Motherhood*. She has written for *Christianity Today* and *Bible Study Magazine*.

Tsuneki Toyoda is instructor of biblical and theological subjects at Rosales Wesleyan Bible College in the Philippines. He received an MS in theology from Asia-Pacific Nazarene Theological Seminary, with a major in biblical studies (Old Testament), and is a PhD student in Old Testament at Asia Graduate School of Theology, Manila.

Michael G. VanZant is professor of biblical literature and Old Testament and coordinator of online Christian ministry programs at Mount Vernon Nazarene University. He is an ordained elder in the Church of the Nazarene and contributor to the *New Interpreter's Dictionary of the Bible*.